FIGHTER MASTER FOLLAND

AND
THE GLADIATORS

FIGHTER MASTER FOLLAND

AND
THE GLADIATORS

DEREK N. JAMES

TEMPUS

For my wife Brenda,
whose encouragement has made this book,
and the previous eighteen, possible.

Frontispiece: On Silver Wings: the pilots of these three Gloster Gladiators of 87 Squadron, Royal Air Force, flew an aerobatic display at Villacoublay in France in July 1938 with their aircraft 'tied-together'.

First published 2007

Tempus Publishing
Cirencester Road, Chalford,
Stroud, Gloucestershire, GL6 8PE
www.tempus-publishing.com

Tempus Publishing is an imprint of NPI Media Group

British Library Cataloguing in Publication Data.
A catalogue record for this book is available from the British Library.

ISBN 978 0 7524 4397 3

Typesetting and origination by NPI Media Group
Printed in Great Britain

CONTENTS

ACKNOWLEDGEMENTS

No author can write a book without the help of others in the twenty-first century. In the eighteenth century John Donne expressed this fact with rather more feeling: 'No man is an Iland, intire of it selfe'. In the year 2000 this author borrowed Donne's words to begin a history of Folland Aircraft and makes no apology for doing so again.

My thanks, then, for their ever ready help, go to Michael Oakey and Nick Stroud, editor and sections editor of *Aeroplane Monthly* respectively, for their support which got the book under way; to fellow author Barry Jones for his inspiring title for this book and to aviation historian Philip Jarrett for the loan of rare photographs; to Brian Riddle, librarian at The Royal Aeronautical Society and Lillian Palmer in the Local Studies and History Department at Birmingham's City Library who provided vital information on Henry Folland's early years in aviation; to Captain Eric Brown RN, the world's most experienced test pilot, for permission to include his amazing reminiscences of flying a Gauntlet, previously published in one of his *Wings of the Weird and Wonderful* books; to Geoff Worrall, Gloster's last chief test pilot, for his memories of some epic flights in the Gladiator; to Chris Hodson, Military Programme Manager of Smiths Aerospace at Hamble who, over many years, has provided me with photographs and information about Folland Aircraft Co.; to Ted Currier, well-known aviation photographer, who came to my aid with numbers of hitherto unpublished photographs, and to Clive Richards at the Ministry of Defence's Air Historical Branch (RAF) who found a copy of the all-important Specification F.7/30 for me; to Terry Holloway at the Marshall Group of Companies who briefed me on his company's unique use of repaired Gladiators during the Second World War, and to Amy Rigg, my publisher at Tempus, who patiently guided me through the intricacies of a new-style contract.

Derek N. James,
Barnwood
Gloucester
September 2007

PROLOGUE

Of the countless types of British aircraft which have filled our skies since 1908, only a handful of comparatively recent vintage are known by name to the general public. Spitfire? a resounding 'Yes!' How about Fury, Brabazon, Harrier or Gauntlet? Hmmm – possibly. Asked to name their principal designers even aviation enthusiasts' brows will furrow as mental data-banks are scanned for a name. On a good day Mitchell, Camm, and Russell are dredged up and possibly Hooper but rarely, if ever, Folland. Yet Henry Folland's designs ran the gamut of aeroplane types. Predominantly fighters, they were built in their thousands for the Royal Flying Corps (RFC), the Royal Air Force (RAF) and thirteen other nation's air forces. But there were also research aircraft, an ultralight and an unmanned flying bomb, racing landplanes and floatplanes, bombers, deck-landing aircraft and trainers.

Folland's first biplane fighter flew in the First World War. His last, which fought in the Second World War, bore the names of the star of an ancient Roman entertainment, a marching tune and of a film. In the spring of 1935 the Air Ministry chose this same name for his new prototype. No name could have been more appropriate than that of the men who, two millennia ago, fought to the death with a *gladius*, which was a short sword. They were the original gladiators. The entry of Henry Folland's Gladiators to RAF squadrons signalled the end of the historic era of biplane fighters that had begun in military aviation's earliest days and which continued until the arrival of the monoplane fighter in the form of the never-to-be-forgotten Hawker Hurricane and Supermarine Spitfire.

It is a long journey from the first twinkle in an aircraft designer's eyes as he envisages his next new aeroplane, to the moment it takes wing, up and away, into its rightful element. For Henry Philip Folland designing, building and flying model aeroplanes were early steps along a twenty-year road into the ranks of the world's leading aircraft-design engineers.

ONE

HENRY PHILIP FOLLAND OBE, FRAeS, FRSA and FIAeS – THE MAN

Eric H.S. Folland, one of Henry Folland's sons, included these words in the inaugural Folland Memorial Lecture, *The Life and Work of H.P. Folland*, before the Gloucester & Cheltenham Branch of the Royal Aeronautical Society on 21 February 1974:

His private life was a very happy one. To my brother and me he was a source of inspiration and unfailing help in times of trouble. When he died I lost a good friend. H.P.F. was a man of great charm, possessing a wonderful sense of humour and a sincere liking for his fellow men. He had high principles and few prejudices, was slow to judge and quick to forgive, a man who made his own way in life, his assets being his immense drive, an inventive mind and a refusal to accept defeat. Although having a 'game' leg he enjoyed golf and was a difficult man to beat at snooker and billiards, which Sir George Dowty confirmed from the many occasions they played together at Cheltenham's Lansdown Hotel in the 1920s and 1930s. Cricket was his great love and he spent many happy hours at the College Ground during the Cheltenham Cricket Festival.

His sense of humour sometimes led him to play practical jokes on his colleagues. With two others he visited the house of a Gloster director and on entering the hall he dropped some kippers into an umbrella hanging on a stand. A subsequent spell of dry, hot weather resulted in a foul smell throughout the house and the Borough Council's sewage department was called in. Despite diligent examinations under floors and down drains the source, surprisingly, was not discovered. It was not until it rained and the umbrella was opened that the mystery was solved. The perpetrator was never discovered.

A long-serving Folland Aircraft employee wrote:

H.P.F. was more like a father than a boss to each and everyone and the happy atmosphere prevalent was never more apparent than during those dark days from 1940 to 1944 when homes were destroyed and a helping hand was sorely needed. Then the guv'ner became a real friend to all in distress and need and his sympathy and understanding of human nature endeared him to each and every one of the staff from the humblest sweeper-up to the executive level alike. To Mr Folland all men were equal and essential to each other and his kindly nature swept away the barriers of class distinction in an endeavour to make each employee feel that he was personally interested in them and their well-being. Here, indeed, was a great man in every sense of the word, whose personality stamped him as a giant among his fellow humans. No pride nor arrogance here, but a friendly down-to-earth human being full of sympathy and understanding for those in his employ.

Sir Roy Fedden, who led Bristol Aeroplane's Engine Division for so many years, commented:

> He had the great gift of leadership. Folland was a very kind and human man. He was always approachable and there are many to whom he gave a helping hand. He was capable of rising to great heights if given the opportunity and inspiration. He inspired loyalty and friendship among his staff but could be difficult and terse with those outside.

Fedden sensed an element of shyness in Folland which may have contributed to the fact that he did not seem to have many friends among the other aircraft designers. However, in the outside world he found time to serve with a number of voluntary organisations and, having seen the benefits that emerged from Gloster Aircraft's apprenticeship schemes, in later life he established one in Folland Aircraft and participated in its development. He also had considerable interest in technical education in schools and colleges in the Gloucester, Cheltenham and Hamble areas.

One wonders what part his ever-present pipe played in his life. Was it for appearance's sake, an appetite suppressor or something to occupy his hands in photographs. Whatever it was, it appears that his pipe rarely left his hand, only to appear in a smoking position.

He remained a member of the Board of Folland Aircraft until his death. on 4 September 1954. His ashes were scattered over Laffan's Plain on the site of the old Royal Aircraft Factory, where he had begun his life as a designer of aeroplanes.

Henry Phillip Folland was always well dressed, but rarely seen without his pipe. His firm gaze assesses the viewer whose attention he holds.

TWO

HERITAGE YEARS

Henry Folland – designer of a series of eighteen types of biplane fighter aircraft over a nineteen-year period culminating in the Gloster Gladiator – was born in Cambridge on 22 January 1889 and left school aged only thirteen. Owing to his interest in motorcars, he later left home and moved to live in Coventry. Once there in 1905, he became an apprentice with the Lanchester Motor Co. Money was short and most of his leisure time was spent either at night school classes in engineering and mathematics or studying technical books borrowed from the local library. During those early years his attention was drawn to aviation and he began designing and flying gliders and elastically powered model aeroplanes.

In 1908, with his indentures secured at the Lanchester Motor Co., he joined the Daimler Motor Co. as a draughtsman. It was whilst at Daimler that the tall twenty-year-old, bespectacled young Folland's inventive mind took wing towards powered flying machines.

Fortuitously, a field almost on Henry Folland's doorstep was to become one of the cradles of British aviation. Henry's son, Eric, told the author that at weekends his father sometimes cycled the ten miles from his Coventry home to Castle Bromwich, near Birmingham, where a playing field had become a flying ground and the home of the recently formed Midland Aero Club. On 24 September 1909, Folland saw pioneer aviator Alfred Pericles Maxfield, an Aston engineer, get airborne in his home-built aeroplane – a glider to which he had added an 18hp three-cylinder engine. Although only a 50ft 'hop' it was the first flight by a powered aircraft built in Birmingham. Aviator B.C. Hucks also visited this site, flying his Bleriot monoplane.

Undoubtedly, these events further stimulated Folland's interest in aeroplanes. He devoted his spare time to studying all of the published information on the theory of flight and aircraft structures that he could lay his hands on. Then, in April 1911, the creation of the Royal Aircraft Factory at Farnborough, followed by the formation of the RFC in May 1912, also silently beckoned him towards the aviation world. Collectively they convinced him that he should take part in this exciting new adventure in the air. Folland was also convinced that Castle Bromwich was not the place to start. But where was the place? Unbeknown to him, the answer was within the Daimler design office.

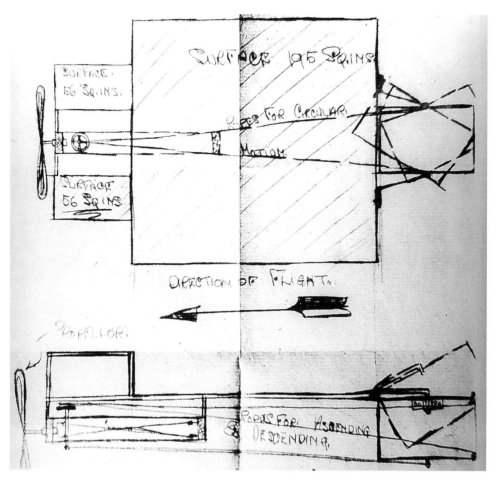

Was this the result of the first aviation twinkle in the eye of the eighteen-year-old Henry Folland? His drawing of an elastic-powered model monoplane with a 195 sq. in area rectangular wing and same shaped control surfaces is dated about 1905. The tail surfaces appear to act both as rudders and elevators. The annotations on the drawing are interesting. 'Ropes for circular motion' and 'Rods for ascending and descending'. The tractor power-unit is in the nose.

THREE

THE ROYAL AIRCRAFT FACTORY

Henry Folland was not the first member of Daimler's design staff to join the Royal Aircraft Factory. Frederick Green, previously one of Daimler's engine design team, had been appointed Engineer-Design at the factory. Thus, in 1912, Folland also quit Daimler and, following in Green's footsteps, moved to Farnborough as a section leader in the Royal Aircraft Factory's design office where he was to become known as 'H.P.F.'

During the ensuing five years, initially in close association with Geoffrey de Havilland and Edward Busk – both test pilots and designers – and other members of the design team at Farnborough, he contributed to the design of several Royal Aircraft Factory aircraft. By now Howard E. Preston, a senior draughtsman and stressman, had teamed up with Folland as his assistant. In addition, Folland had shared with de Havilland the design of the B.S.1, (Bleriot Scout), the world's first single-seat scout or fighter. This first flew on 13 March 1913 and was rebuilt, following a crash, as the S.E.2. (Scouting Experimental).

Although Folland's early designs were influenced to some degree by cost of production plus economy and ease of maintenance and operation, it must be said at once that, throughout his life, Folland would never take for himself the sole credit or the glory for a successful design. Eric Folland told the author that his father had said to him: 'Successful design is a team proposition, not a one-man job.'

Folland had also done some preliminary design work on the S.E.3, a project which, fortunately, was abandoned in favour of his first accredited design for the S.E.4 high-speed aircraft in 1914. This was not a military aeroplane, simply one designed to achieve the highest possible speed with safety; it was, in effect, a low-cost tool – or toy – with which the Royal Aircraft Factory's aerodynamicists and pilots could play and put theories into practice!

The S.E.4 was powered by a fully cowled Gnome 160hp fourteen-cylinder, twin-row, air-cooled Lambda-Lambda rotary engine having a large pot-shaped propeller spinner. The fuselage had the conventional, internally wire-braced, four-longeron wooden structure with formers clad with plywood panels to create an oval cross section. The wooden fabric-covered biplane wings were not staggered and, to minimise drag, had single I-section struts with wide-chord top and bottom attachments to the front and rear spars.

It is interesting to note that, while the contemporary Avro 511 had fabricated wide chord structures described as single inter-plane struts, Folland's strut design was not copied until, during the 1916–17 'rush for much' in wing area, Frederic Koolhoven's

Armstrong Whitworth F.K.9 and 10 Quadruplanes, Reinhold Platz's Fokker Dr.I triplane and the Sopwith triplane – probably designed by Hawker, Herbert Smith and Sopwith – had this type of strut.

Returning to Folland's S.E.4: the single centre-section struts, of similar configuration, were hollow and it was through these that the control cables to the four full-span ailerons were routed. These surfaces could be lowered together to act as landing flaps. The cruciform tail unit embodied dorsal and ventral fins which, like the single I-section interplane struts, were to become a Folland 'signature' feature that would appear on many of his fighter designs. When first built, the landing gear had streamlined struts arranged as an inverted tripod carrying a transverse leaf spring at its lower end, to which the wheels were attached. After initial flight testing in June 1914 by Royal Aircraft Factory test pilot Norman Spratt, this landing gear was considered to be insufficiently stiff. Spratt complained to Folland that this caused the aircraft to rock from side-to-side when taxiing, so Preston produced drawings for a more conventional pair of vee-struts with a cross axle attached by bungee rubber chords. Another modification was a hole cut in the nose of the spinner to admit more cooling air to the engine which was continually overheating.

As will be seen, Folland's economic no-risk design philosophy, which he clung to almost throughout his life as a designer, was evolution rather than revolution; moreover, he was always looking for 'aerodynamic purity' in his designs that incorporated many features aimed at minimising drag. Thus, in addition to those described above in the S.E.4, he designed a streamlined celluloid canopy which was to be fitted over the cockpit. Unfortunately, none of the Farnborough test pilots, including de Havilland, liked the idea of being enclosed and this unique piece of equipment was never flight tested.

Due to overheating and other problems with the 160hp Gnome engine a much less powerful Gnome Delta 110hp nine-cylinder, single-row engine was installed, which reduced the S.E.4's top speed from 135mph to 95mph. Nevertheless, this little aeroplane, now in a coat of camouflage and with the serial number 628, was handed over to the RFC. Although the S.E.4's 50mph landing speed was reckoned to be 'a bit too quick' for squadron pilots, its general flying characteristics were acceptable. Understandably, this S.E.4 never flew operationally. It was damaged beyond repair in an accident in August 1914 when the starboard wheel collapsed after a tyre burst during what could have been an example of those 'too quick' landings.

Although the designation S.E.4a gives the impression that this Folland-designed aeroplane was a development of its predecessor, aside from the general configuration only the full-span ailerons and tailplane stemmed from it. New features included a cowled Gnome 80hp engine, metal tube longerons forward of the cockpit, twin-interplane struts, the upper wings joining on the centreline on inverted vee struts and dihedral on both wings. In addition, the fabric-covered S.E.4a was built as another 'tool' for a Royal Aircraft Establishment (RAE) research programme covering manoeuvrability and stability. Frank Gooden, a Farnborough test pilot, first flew the S.E.4a prototype on 25 June 1915.

With small modifications and a gun on top of the upper wing's centre-line joint so that it fired over the propeller disc, three more S.E.4as were built for the RFC. Two were serialled 5610 and 5611, but the third serial cannot be confirmed. For a short period in October 1915, one S.E.4a belonging to No.6 Wing, RFC, was attached to Joyce Green

Airfield near Dartford, Kent, for Home Defence duties. For a brief period Folland's research 'tool' had become an aerial weapon. In 1916, some twenty-eight years before Nazi Germany's V.1 Doodle-bug unguided weapons were launched against Britain during the Second World War, Folland was given responsibility for the design of a remote-controlled flying bomb. Powered by an A.B.C. 35hp two-cylinder Gnat engine turning a small wooden propeller, six bombs were built. For secrecy and political reasons, they were categorised as aerial targets. None managed to remain airborne long enough for the radio-control system to be activated and the programme was abandoned.

Undoubtedly, it was the design of the S.E.5 in 1916, and the S.E.5a a year later – for which Folland had principal responsibility – that signalled his arrival in the front rank of aircraft designers. Almost certainly there would have been some design input by the Royal Aircraft Factory test pilots and certainly from Howard Preston. Its conventional structure was created around the excellent 200hp geared eight-cylinder, vee in-line liquid-cooled Type A engine produced by Hispano-Suiza, a company whose name reflects the Spanish site and the Swiss engineer, Marc Birkigt, who established his first factory there.

To meet the Air Board's requirements the S.E.5's design features included a simple, wooden, internally wire-braced, box-structure fuselage with five rounded-top formers supporting stringers to give shape to the fabric covering. Wooden decking surrounded the cockpit and forward section. A large rectangular radiator was mounted in front of the engine with the fuel tank behind it on the top longerons. The tail unit was almost an exact copy of the S.E.4. The single-bay, internally wire-braced fabric-covered wings were staggered and were built around two spruce spars. The parallel-chord wings had four ailerons for good manoeuvrability, a generous near-five-degree dihedral for stability and the tailplane incidence could be adjusted in flight. All the control surface cables were routed internally. Three prototypes, numbered A4561–63, were built, but as Hispano-Suiza had failed to deliver any 200hp engines, 150hp direct-drive units were installed instead. The first unarmed S.E.5 was first flown by Frank Gooden on 22 November 1916. It is recorded that, after landing, Folland asked him how it handled in the air. 'She's a pixie,' replied Gooden.

During its development, which included operational trials with RFC squadrons in France, the S.E.5 was flown with several different Hispano-Suiza engines and their licence-built derivative the Wolseley Viper engine. A number of airframe modifications also were embodied. Armament was a .303in Vickers gun partially enclosed in the nose on the port side and pointing slightly above the line of flight to counteract bullet drop over an increased range. The synchronising gear system in the S.E.5, which allowed the gun to fire through the propeller disc, could only cope with one gun; thus, a same-calibre Lewis gun was carried on a special Foster mounting high on the upper-centre section clear of the propeller. This gun was mounted on a down-curved rail, rather like a hockey stick, so that it could be lowered in flight to enable the pilot to fit new ammunition pans. Once lowered, however, it took the strength of Hercules to push it back up onto the centre section. Some early S.E.5s had a large 'greenhouse' windscreen to protect the pilot while he wrestled with this gun and its heavy fully loaded ammunition pans. However, smaller windscreens soon replaced it. A total of forty-eight production S.E.5s were built at Farnborough and flew with 56 and 60 Squadrons in France.

S.E.5a Squadrons

When pilots discovered some snags in the S.E.5 the third prototype was modified to overcome them. Powered by the 200hp geared Hispano Suiza engine it was designated the S.E.5a and was highly praised by RFC test pilots. Large orders were placed, not only with the RAE but with five other manufacturers who between them produced a total of 5,180 S.E.5as. During the First World War the S.E.5 and 5a equipped some thirty RFC and RAF squadrons in the UK and France. Four of these squadrons also operated in Macedonia, Palestine, Syria and Egypt.

Numbers of modifications were embodied as squadron pilots and ground crews weeded out minor problems during operational flying. Many aircraft were personalised by squadron engineers to suit individual pilots' requirements; different seat heights, modified cockpit cut outs, even an extra gun firing downwards from the cockpit – though this was removed very soon after its first firing! They were flown against enemy bomber and fighter formations but also in the ground-attack role carrying light bombs. Folland's little biplane was considered by many pilots to be the best British single-seat fighter and at least five of the nineteen RFC pilots who received the Victoria Cross during the war scored many of their victories while flying the S.E.5 and 5a. One of those pilots, Major James McCudden VC, of 56 Squadron, was high in its praise: 'The S.E.5a which I was now flying was a most efficient fighting machine, far and away superior to the enemy machines of that period'. He referred particularly to its great strength, its diving and zooming powers and excellent view: 'Apart from this it was a warm, comfortable and easy machine to fly. German pilots who had become prisoners considered the S.E.5a a most formidable fighting machine'. After the war this battle-proven aircraft type continued to serve in RAF squadrons until early 1920.

An SE.4 with the original inverted tripod landing gear. Note the pierced spinner, single interplane and centre-section struts and strutted tailplane.

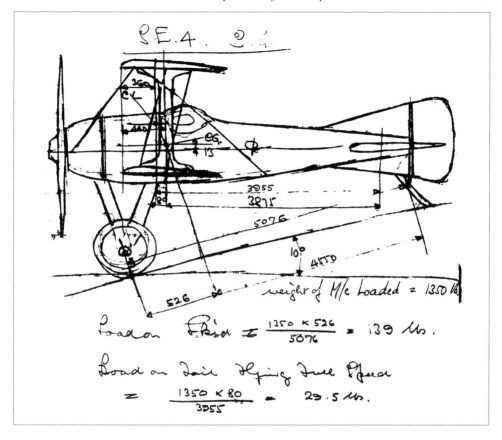

An SE.4 stressing diagram to assess the load on the tail when flying at full speed. Although the measurements appear to be metric the sum at the bottom gives the Imperial answer 29.5lb. The cockpit canopy is an interesting design feature.

The SE.4's inverted tripod and leaf spring landing gear.

A camouflaged SE.4 serialled 628 on its rudder. It is believed that this photograph was taken before 628 took-off on its last flight with the Royal Flying Corps.

Photographed on 12 August 1914 SE.4 628 lies inverted after its starboard tyre burst during a fast landing. The pilot survived.

A4561, the first prototype SE.5 at Farnborough with Frank Gooden in the cockpit for its first flight on 22 November 1916.

The first SE.5 is man-handled into position for a flight a few days after it first got airborne. Note the one-outlet exhaust manifold.

A rare air-to-air photograph of an unidentifiable SE.5 with the steel-tube landing gear, built-up fuselage aft of the cockpit and an enlarged windscreen.

Built by Wolseley Motors in Birmingham and serialled F904, this SE.5a was stored at Whitley from 1928 until 1956 before restoration. Now with the Shuttleworth Collection as D7000 it flies low during a rehearsal at Farnborough.

SE.5a D7000 appeared in the SBAC Flying Display at Farnborough on four occasions during the 1960s. Here, with its engine running, it is being prepared for a flight.

A magnificent study of F904/D7000 in a shimmering aluminium/silver finish at an Open Day at RAF Upavon on 13 May 1962 marking the fiftieth anniversary of the founding of the Royal Flying Corps.

FOUR

NIEUPORT & GENERAL AIRCRAFT

Surprisingly, during 1917, about mid-way through the First World War, the Royal Aircraft Factory underwent some major changes in remit and organisation following claims by British aircraft manufacturers that the Factory was competing with them for Government contracts. These and other changes resulted in the Factory's designers becoming disgruntled with the general organisation there and numbers of them left Farnborough and moved to private aircraft manufacturers. Among them was twenty-eight-year-old Henry Folland who moved with his young family to live in Dollis Hill near Willesden Green when he joined the Nieuport & General Co. Ltd at Cricklewood, which had been looking for a designer of its own.

Not long after leaving Farnborough, Folland was joined at Cricklewood by Howard Preston who was to work with Folland for the majority of his life.

The first design for their new employer was the B.N.1, a chunky twin-bay three-gun biplane fighter intended to meet Air Board Specification A.1A as a replacement for the Sopwith Camel scout. At first sight, with its upper wing close to the fuselage, it looked a bit like an Airfix kit which had been slightly sat upon! Its I-section interplane and centre-section struts, ventral fin and upper-wing-mounted gun echoed those of the S.E.4 and S.E.5. Three prototype B.N.1s, with early examples of the Bentley 230hp nine-cylinder B.R.2 air-cooled rotary engine, were ordered. Serialled C3484-86, the first one flew in February 1918. The following month it went to the RFC's Aeroplane Experimental Unit (AEU) at Martlesham Heath, Suffolk, where it recorded a 128mph top speed. Sadly, it crashed in flames near Sutton Bridge, Lincolnshire, on 10 March and as both of the two other prototypes were still being built, the type was withdrawn from the trials. When the second B.N.1 was completed it was used for static structural-strength tests, but the third was scrapped.

Folland followed the B.N.1 design with the Nighthawk fighter which was intended to meet an Air Board Specification. Unfortunately, this made mandatory the use of the A.B.C. Motors's Dragonfly, a disastrous radial engine. Designed by Granville Bradshaw – a born salesman who also firmly believed himself to be a skilled design engineer – the result was that the Dragonfly, when running, not only overheated to such a degree that parts of it became red hot but was also overweight. It never delivered the quoted power and usually broke its crankshaft after an hour or two's running.

The sole Nieuport BN.1 fighter which first flew in February 1918 and crashed in March. Folland 'trade-mark' features include the I-section interplane struts, and the neat engine installation.

The second prototype Nighthawk, F2910, seen on 18 June 1918 at Cricklewood. Its tail unit is a copy of the BN.1

The 21st 'production' Nieuport-built Nighthawk. Note the Dragonfly engine, fabric-covered rear fuselage and heavily wire-braced wing cellule. It was flown at the Aeroplane Experimental Establishment, Martlesham Heath, during 1920–21.

A standard Dragonfly-powered Nieuport Nighthawk.

This Nighthawk made Britain's first commercial delivery of newspapers by aircraft. On 14 March 1919 at 6.25 a.m. the late edition of the *Daily Mail* left Acton Aerodrome and it was in the hands of the Mayor of Bournemouth, still in his pyjamas, at 7.15 a.m. This was 45 minutes before other London papers had reached the town.

In a bright blue and yellow chequered racing finish the Nieuhawk racer and demonstration aircraft, basically a Nighthawk with a much modified Dragonfly engine, had a 151mph top speed.

Civil Registered G-EASK, the Goshawk had a very streamlined and effective installation for its similarly modified Dragonfly and Folland had reverted to single I-section interplane struts.

Using various design features from both the S.E.5a and B.N.1 and with ease of manufacture in mind, Folland created the Nighthawk. A tidy two-bay biplane fighter, it embodied a number of S.E.5a components and a B.N.1 tail unit. In April 1918 – a long time before the Dragonfly's reliability could be established – three Nighthawk prototypes, F2909–11, were ordered to meet Air Board Specification A.1(C), which was later to be amalgamated with the RAF Type 1 Specification. As further evidence of the Air Ministry's misplaced faith in Mr Bradshaw and his Dragonfly, the Nieuport & General Co. received an order for 150 Nighthawks long before flight-approved examples of the Dragonfly had become available for the prototypes.

The first Nighthawk prototype, serialled F2910, probably flew in the early spring of 1919 before going to the Aeroplane Experimental Station (as it was then named) at Martlesham Heath for airframe and engine evaluation in June. With the September 1919 cancellation of a vast order for the problem-riddled Dragonfly – by which time about 1,200 had been produced and put into to store – numbers of Nighthawks were re-engined with Armstrong Siddeley Jaguar or Bristol Aeroplane Jupiter engines. Although a batch of 286 Nighthawks had been ordered, only seventy had Dragonfly engines. Of this number Nieuport & General Co. had subcontracted thirty to the comparatively recently formed Gloucestershire Aircraft Co. Ltd at Sunningend in Cheltenham. The first Nieuport-built Nighthawk airframe to be modified by Gloucestershire Aircraft Co. was sent to the RAE at Farnborough in November 1920 before going on to Martlesham Heath in the following year.

In addition, a further fifty-four engineless airframes were assembled, about a dozen being transferred to the Cheltenham factory plus stocks of components. The rest of the batch were cancelled. Out of this shambles would come a number of Nighthawks for use by the RAE, the Marine Aircraft Experimental Establishment at Felixstowe and Martlesham's renamed Aeroplane Experimental Establishment.

When he had first conceived this Nighthawk design Henry Folland could not have foreseen the ways in which he, ably supported by Howard Preston, would modify and adapt the basic airframe to create a series of military and civil aeroplanes. In 1919, with Nighthawk components still littering the Cricklewood factory, Folland – almost as a sideline – designed a two-seater variant and the single-seater Nieuhawk racer, both with much-modified A.B.C. 320hp Dragonfly engines that were almost given away. The two-seater variant ended its days in India, flying newspapers from Bombay to Poona. The following year he also designed the trim Goshawk racing biplane; it had single broad-chord, inter-plane struts, a carefully faired, almost cylindrical-section fuselage and a Dragonfly engine. It was to set a British speed record at 166.5mph. Then, as if to show his versatility, he designed the big London twin-engined triplane bomber, described as a 'flying bomb box' because its fuselage was clad with half-inch-thick wooden tongued-and-grooved match boarding! Both were built as one-offs.

FIVE

GLOUCESTERSHIRE AIRCRAFT COMPANY'S MARS SERIES

Back in early 1915, when the Aircraft Manufacturing Co. (Airco) at Hendon was seeking a subcontractor to help with the production of D.H.2 fighter components, it had been directed to H.H. Martyn & Co. Ltd at Sunningend in Cheltenham. Widely renowned in the architectural-engineering field it had an established reputation for first-class woodwork, particularly for its wood panelling in ocean liners, a skilled work force and a well-equipped factory. During the remaining three years of the First World War some 700 aircraft – designed by Geoffrey de Havilland at Airco and by Frank Barnwell at British & Colonial Aircraft Co. at Bristol – were produced under subcontract at the Sunningend factory. Meanwhile, in June 1917, Gloucestershire Aircraft Co. Ltd was formed to rent Martyn's production facilities and take over this subcontract work.

At the war's end when military aircraft production ceased and H.H. Martyn struggled to obtain work back in its own field, Gloucestershire Aircraft Co. boldly decided to stay in the aviation business. However, although the Nieuport company's fortunes began to slide following swingeing cancellations of war-time contracts, it managed to keep the wolf from the hangar doors and it was not until 1921 that it finally closed for business at Cricklewood. By then Gloucestershire Aircraft Co. had taken its first steps towards its goal of becoming an independent aircraft manufacturer. Having earlier built a number of Nieuport Nighthawks under subcontract it acquired the design and production rights to this fighter and acquired a large quantity of surplus Nighthawk airframes and components. The Cheltenham company also engaged the part-time services of Henry Folland as a three-days-a-week consultant to oversee the development of this aeroplane for further production in its Sunningend factory.

Folland's first part-time design for Gloucestershire Aircraft Co. was the Mars MkI Bamel racer created in just four weeks in early 1921. Drawing heavily on the S.E.4, it was powered by a Napier 450hp Lion twelve-cylinder, broad-arrow, in-line, liquid-cooled engine. This aircraft's design features included broad-chord single interplane struts, a Nighthawk tail unit, some linen covering on its spoked wheels and re-styled wings. It set a British Airspeed Record at 196.4mph in December 1921 and won the Aerial Derby in the same year and again in 1922. The aircraft – with modifications as the Gloster MkI – won again in 1923. In 1921 and 1922 it flew in the Coupe Deutsch race at Villesauvage

Above: A poor but historic photograph taken in 1919 of a partly completed Nighthawk in the Sunningend factory. From left are H. Jeanes (labourer), Hubert Martyn (A.W. Martyn's nephew), H. Munn (foreman) and G. Shepherd (charge hand).

Right: Hugh Burroughes, a founding director of Gloucestershire Aircraft Co., who encouraged Henry Folland to join the company as its designer in August 1921.

in France; sadly, little hiccups like wing-fabric failure and maps blown overboard twice robbed the little racer of a victory. The name 'Bamel' came from a chance remark made when Hugh Burroughes, a founding director of the company, first went with Folland to see the aircraft under construction. Burroughes told the author: 'Only the front section of the fuselage was covered while the rear was still bare. Folland commented that in that state, with the large hump of the fuel tank up front it was "half bear and half camel" which produced Bamel!' This hybrid beast, with a bear's hindquarters and, with Jimmy James, its pilot, aboard wearing a flowing white scarf, was adopted as an unofficial racing motif. It should be noted that with very few exceptions, Folland's fighter designs had fabric-covered wings, tail units and rear fuselages – only the front fuselage section being clad with metal panels and cowlings.

In July 1921 soon after the Mars MkI Bamel first became airborne, Henry Folland joined Gloucestershire Aircraft Co. as chief engineer and designer. Not surprisingly, he was accompanied by Howard Preston as his assistant. Headlines in *The Gloucestershire Echo* evening newspaper reported, 'Bamel's designer goes west to make Sparrowhawks in Gloucestershire' and 'The man who made too fast a machine'. Its Air Correspondent wrote: 'An event of far-reaching importance takes place today when Mr H.P. Folland, the king of racing-aircraft designers, definitely severs his connection with the British Nieuport Co. and joins Gloucestershire Aircraft.' *Flight* magazine stated: 'The Gloucestershire Aircraft Co. may for the moment not be so well known. This is a shortcoming which, under Mr Folland's technical leadership will, no doubt, soon be remedied.' Within a few weeks supervised by Folland, modification work began on the Bamel.

Using the Nieuport Nighthawk as a basis Folland then produced designs for three variants named Mars MkII, III and IV: they were built specially to meet an order from the Imperial Japanese Navy. These were to be Folland's first fighter designs for Gloucestershire Aircraft Co. Renamed Sparrowhawk, they were powered by Bentley 150hp B.R.2 nine-cylinder, air-cooled rotary engines. A mixed batch of fifty of these aeroplanes was ordered and built in 1921 as the Sparrowhawk MkI single-seater land-based fighters, Sparrowhawk MkII two-seater fighter trainers and the Sparrowhawk MkIII ship-borne fighters. In addition, the contract covered the supply to Japan of forty complete ship-sets of Sparrowhawk spares and components.

The Sparrowhawk MkIII's landing-gear axle fairing were modified to carry jaws to suit the longitudinal cable deck-arrester system then in use on aircraft carriers; a hydrovane was mounted on the front of the landing gear to prevent the aircraft from nosing-over if it had to alight in the sea and floatation bags were carried in the fuselage. For operations from warships at sea wooden platforms, some 40ft long, were mounted on top of the gun turrets of several Japanese warships. The platforms could be turned into wind and slightly elevated with the guns. The Sparrowhawks were secured to these platforms which had a quick-release hook which engaged with the landing gear. For take-off the engine was run at full-throttle and the hook was then slipped on a signal from the pilot. All these aircraft served with the Japanese naval air units until 1928.

The Mars MkVI Nighthawk was, in effect, a modified Nieuport aeroplane re-engined with either an Armstrong Siddeley Jaguar MkII or Bristol Jupiter MkIII, both 325hp air-cooled radial engines. It was Folland's fifth Nighthawk variant. Differences from the Nieuport design included full-length fuselage fairings which gave the aeroplane a neat

This photograph, taken at Sunningend, shows the fine lines of the Mars I Bamel and its high-gloss paint finish. Large ailerons were fitted only on the lower wings. The broad-chord single inter-plane struts and careful attention to detail design produced a minimum-drag airframe for the Mars I.

Note the coolant pipe linking the Mars I's centre-section radiator and the engine, the different wing shapes and the close-cowled Lion engine.

This close-up view of James in the Mars I Bamel reveals the 'half-bear half-camel' motif below the cockpit.

The crated and tarpaulin-wrapped Mars I's wings and fuselage, en route to Villesauvage in France where it flew in the Coupe Deutsch de la Meurthe contest in September 1921.

A large crowd of French enthusiasts eye the Mars I at Villesauvage in 1921 with Jimmy James in the cockpit. Despite the Contest number on the rudder another one, hastily applied, appeared necessary.

G-EAXZ at the Aeroplane Experimental Establishment at Martlesham Heath where it set a new 196.4mph British Speed Record in December 1921.

well-rounded streamlined shape and the use of a number of metal fuselage and wing components. Ailerons were carried on upper and lower wings and the tailplane incidence could be altered in flight by screw jacks and a cable actuation system. The armament was two .303in Vickers machine guns carried on the top of the front fuselage with an interrupter system which allowed them to fire through the propeller disc from each side of the Jupiter engine's top cylinder or squeezing between the Jaguar's twin rows of cylinders. In this way their breeches were within easy reach of the pilot who could bash them with a wooden mallet in the event of a stoppage!

To improve its performance for the 1922 Coupe Deutsch contest the Mars I had smaller wings, a larger SE.5 style tail unit and linen bags to streamline its wheels.

James taxies the glossy blue and white Mars I to the start line for the 1922 Coupe Deutsche.

With improved wing sections, internal fuel tank to improve forward view and strutted centre-section, in 1923 the Mars I became the Gloster I.

The first Mars II/Sparrowhawk I single-seat land-based fighter-scout for the Imperial Japanese Navy at Hucclecote. Folland's adaption of the Nighthawk is very apparent.

JN401 was the first Mars MkIII/Sparrowhawk MkII two-seat trainer for Japan's naval cadet pilots.

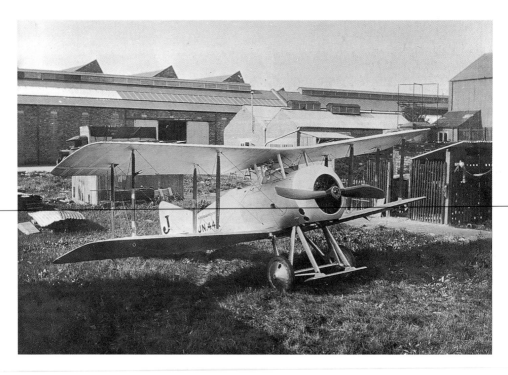

Mars IV/Sparrowhawk MkIII, JN442 was the first of the single-seat ship-borne fighters. Seen in the cluttered factory yard at Sunningend, it has a hydrovane attachment on its landing gear.

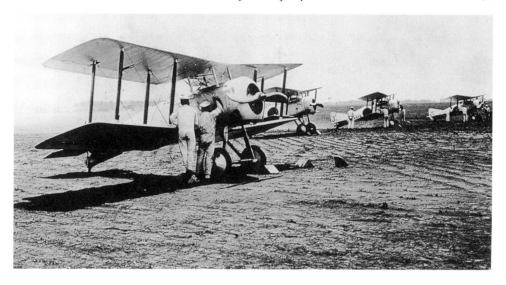

Sparrowhawks on Japan's Kasumigaura Naval Aerodrome. A Sparrowhawk MkII is in the front with some Sparrowhawk Is in the background.

A Sparrowhawk MkIII is flown off a wooden platform mounted on the guns of a Japanese battleship. The hydrofoil does not appear to be fitted.

A Gloucestershire Mars VI Nighthawk at Hucclecote. Note the large propeller boss blending into the Jupiter engine's cowling and the slender landing gear legs.

The second of a small group of three Nighthawk-to-Mars VI conversions, J6926 shows the dihedral on wings and the bracing wire system.

Opposite middle: This view of Mars VI, J6926, at Hucclecote in November 1922, reveals the shape of the fuselage. It flew on engine trials at RAF bases in Iraq and Egypt in 1923–24.

Opposite bottom: The first of a 12 batch of Mars X Nightjars, on 18 December 1922. J6930 had engine failure on take-off for delivery to the AEE, Martlesham Heath, and spun in trying to return to Hucclecote Aerodrome.

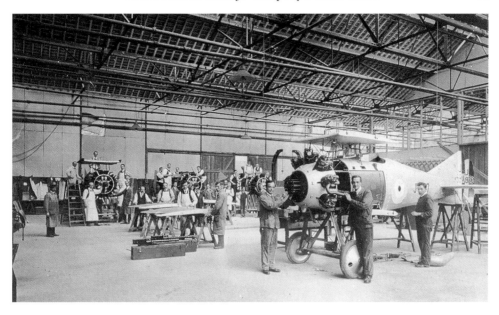

Nieuport Nighthawks being converted to Mars VI Nighthawks and Mars X Nightjars at Gloucestershire Aircraft's Sunningend Works. The aircraft on the right became a Mars VI Nighthawk.

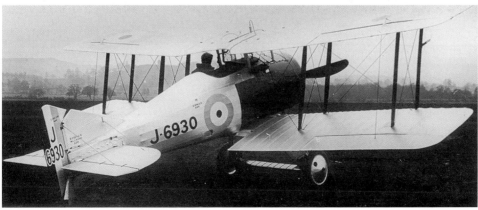

H8539, a Mars X Nightjar seen at RAE Farnborough during 1922. Note the deck-arrester jaws on the wide track landing gear.

The wreckage of a Mars X Nightjar of 402 Flight based at RAF Leuchars which crashed on 2 May 1923.

Nighthawk and Nightjar Squadrons

Although differing records show that Gloucestershire Aircraft Co. created between thirty and sixty Mars MkVI Nighthawks, they also show that only six were taken on charge by the RAF. Three of these were flown by 1, 8, 55 and 208 Squadrons on service trials at Hinaidi, India, during 1923/24.

In 1922 the Greek Government bought twenty-five Jaguar-powered Mars MkVI Nighthawks for the Greek Army Air Force fighter squadrons. Quickly produced in three months, they reached Salonika early in 1923. Issued first to E Fighter Squadron, then to A Aircraft Squadron, which became A Aircraft Regiment, they remained in service until 1938. They were then relegated to training duties.

The final Nighthawk derivative was the Mars X Nightjar which Folland developed as a single-seat deck-landing fighter. It was the first aircraft of this type to see service in British aircraft carriers after the end of the First World War. With an eye to economy, because there were large numbers of Bentley B.R.2 rotary engines surplus to requirements in store, he embodied it in the Nightjar design. With very few airframe changes from the basic Nighthawk being required, as a rapid means of providing the RAF with a naval-type aircraft for operating off aircraft carriers, a batch of twenty-two Nighthawk airframes were converted by Gloucestershire Aircraft Co. Enough airframes and components to serve as spares for twelve Nightjars were also held in stock. Modifications included a wide-track, long-stroke landing gear with deck-arrester jaws but the armament was mounted externally on the front fuselage. During a brief service career which began in June 1922, when the first Nightjar was delivered to 203 Squadron, the following September six were taken in crates aboard the aircraft carrier HMS *Argus* to the Dardanelles where they operated during the Chanak Crisis. When the Fleet Air Arm was formed in April 1924 it took over all the Nightjars which subsequently served with 401, 403 and 404 Flights in carriers HMS *Argus*, *Hermes* and *Furious* respectively.

The missing Mars numbers in this series were the Mars MkV, a two-seat fighter project with a metal-structured fuselage and the Mars MkVIII and MkIX transport projects which had a folding rear fuselage to enable bulky loads to be accommodated.

SIX

FOLLAND'S G-FIGHTERS

The Grebe

The 1923 two-seat Grouse research/trainer, which stemmed from the Sparrowhawk trainer, never entered quantity production; in fact it was a one-off which was to spawn a number of subsequent designs for single-seat fighters. As a private venture design it was originally conceived by Henry Folland for use in flight trials of a special combination of different upper- and lower-wing sections which he had developed to combine the merits of biplane and monoplane configurations. These were known as the Gloster H.L.B (High Lift Biplane) sections for which the company obtained Patent No.225.257, describing it:

> The top plane of a biplane is a thick high-lift section and the bottom plane is of normal section. The outer ends of the top plane are tapered in thickness for about one-fifth of the span and the thickness is also reduced towards the centre in the region of the propeller slipstream, both giving slightly reduced resistance. Ailerons are provided in which the chord increases towards the wing tips for better control.

In the Grouse, which now carried the civil registration G-EAYN, Folland used a relatively thick high-lift upper-wing section, the H.L.B 1, with a normal low-drag lower section, the H.L.B.2. This combination was reckoned to combine a biplane's high-lift for take-off and landing with a monoplane's efficiency and low drag at high speed. This enabled a short wingspan to be used, which when coupled with a short fuselage produced a very agile aeroplane.

For economy the Grouse was designed and built around a modified two-seat Sparrowhawk MkII fuselage with a Bentley 230hp B.R.2 rotary engine. Although the Grouse held no interest for the RAF as a trainer, following a special flight demonstration before Air Ministry top brass at RAF Hendon – which proved Folland's claims for his wing section combination quite convincingly – a contract soon landed on a desk at Gloucestershire Aircraft Co. It instructed the company to proceed with the construction of three prototypes. Strangely identified in the contract as 'The Thick Winged Nighthawk', they were to be powered by Armstrong Siddeley 350hp Jaguar MkIII twin-row, fourteen-cylinder, air-cooled radial engines. In this form the first, serialled J6969, became the prototype Grebe Mk I fighter. It was also the first Folland-designed fighter for Gloucestershire Aircraft Co. to be built in quantity for the RAF, a total of

The home of Folland's G-Fighters, Gloucestershire and Gloster Aircraft Co's Sunningend factory. Note the word 'Aerodrome' on the roof and the arrow pointing to Hucclecote, Gloucester.

Having moved from Dollis Hill following the virtual closure of Nieuport and General Aircraft at Cricklewood, Henry Folland and his wife, Muriel, enjoy the sunshine in the garden of their new home in Hatherley Road, Cheltenham.

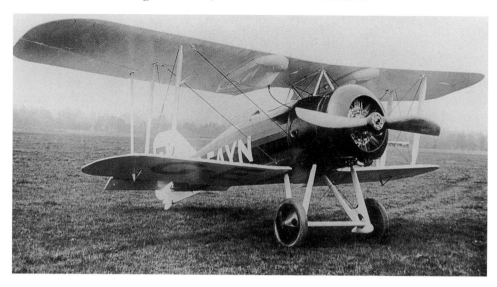

G-EAYN, the Grouse I, had a modified Sparrowhawk II fuselage, a Bentley BR.2 rotary engine with Folland's H.L.B. wing section combination. Note the upper wing's long overhang outboard of the interplane strut.

129 Grebes valued at £313,000, being built in six production batches that also included twenty two-seat trainers. The Grebe occupies a special niche in British aviation history, being the first of the post-First World War generation of fighters to enter RAF service.

The production standard aircraft was designated the Grebe MkII; its near-traditional fuselage structure was built up with ash longerons and spruce struts joined by metal fittings, internally wire-braced and with formers and stringers to provide shape. The wide use of wood in aircraft structures was second nature to the Gloucestershire Aircraft Co. work force, large numbers of whom were skilled 'chippies'. The Armstrong Siddeley 400hp Jaguar MkIV air-cooled radial engine was carried on steel tube bearers attached to the front face of a thick plywood bulkhead. The tail unit was almost identical in shape to those on the S.E.5a and Nighthawk and the tailplane incidence could be adjusted in flight. The single-bay wings had spruce spars and N-girder ribs braced internally by metal tie-rods and the two ailerons on each side, which were hinged on false spars mounted at an angle to the main spars, were interconnected by a solid rod. Fuel was carried in a pair of 26-gallon gravity tanks in the upper wings which joined on the aircraft's centre line. Folland used this location for fuel tanks in many of his designs. All the control surfaces were operated through internal cable systems. The cross-axle main landing gear had vee steel tubes with oleo shock absorbers on the front struts and the tail skid was steerable. Fabric covering was used throughout except for plywood cockpit decking and aluminium panels on the front fuselage section. Two synchronised .303in Vickers machine guns firing through the propeller disc were carried in the top of the front fuselage each with 600 rounds of ammunition; in addition a light bomb-carrier could be fitted under the fuselage with four 20lb bombs.

The first of twelve Grebe MkIIs – serialled J7283 and ordered in Contract 468248/23, dated March 1924 and built to Specification 37/23 – flew its maiden flight in August 1923 and went to the AEE Martlesham Heath for performance trials two months later. With a

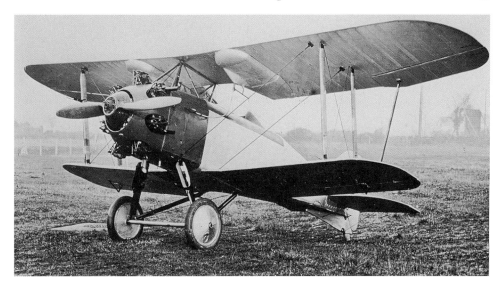

G-EAYN modified as the Grouse II two-seater, had an Armstrong Siddeley Lynx radial engine and an oleo landing gear.

top speed of 162mph the Grebe MkII proved to be a very frisky little aeroplane which, too often for safety's sake, exhibited bird-like tendencies and fluttered its upper wing. The root cause appeared to be the wing's three-foot overhang outboard of the inter-plane strut. It was all too easy for even an experienced pilot to loose a wing as well as his life. The cure was a pair of vee struts between the lower front spar and both spars in the upper wing's overhanging section.

During its flying life the Grebe was involved in three unique events. It was the first aircraft to be tested in a 240mph terminal velocity dive at the AEE and to have survived. There was no sign of wing flutter, only a few stretched bracing wires and control cables marking this test. An interesting feature of this brave and remarkable feat was that although test pilots were not usually provided with parachutes at that time, on this occasion the Grebe's Martlesham pilot, Flight Lieutenant D'Arcy Greig, wore a US-designed Irvin parachute, numbers of which were becoming available.

Secondly, at the 1925 RAF Pageant at Hendon a pair of 25 Squadron Grebes gave a spectacular display of air drill and synchronised aerobatics. The unusual feature of this display was that through the magic of radio-telephony – though installed in some service aircraft it was very much still in its infancy – HM King George V directed some of the Grebes' manoeuvres from the ground.

Thirdly, it was in October 1926 that Folland, aided by the trusty Preston, was called upon to design modifications to two Grebes – J7385 and J7400 – for some air-launching experiments. These aeroplanes, which had quick-release attachments mounted on their upper wings, were slung below the keel member of the British rigid-airship R-33. Their engines were connected by 'elephant's trunk' piping to Bristol gas starters in the airship. After an ascent from Pulham in Norfolk Flying Officer R.L. Ragg's aircraft was released at 2,500ft and flew for several minutes before landing back at Pulham. Flying

Having been sold to Sweden in December 1925, the Grouse II is seen in the markings of the Swedish Army Air Service.

The prototype Grebe, J6969, at Farnborough, with the Folland 'signature' tail unit. This Grebe carries the number 14, its racing number for the 1923 King's Cup Air Race.

With ground crew keeping the tail down, G-EBHA, the Grebe demonstrator aircraft, runs its Armstrong Siddeley Jaguar IIIa engine at the 1923 RAF Air Pageant at Hendon.

Test pilot Larry Carter 'reads the small print' while Henry Folland, with hands in pockets, pipe smoker Capt Gordon Charley, and overseas sales director with company secretary Charles Denley, await the arrival of the Infante of Spain at Hucclecote during the early 1920s.

Immaculately dressed, Folland and Capt Charley are pictured with the Spanish Infante and his son at the Sunningend factory.

The first Grebe II, J7283, spent most of its flying life as a trials aircraft at the A&AEE and with 25 and 56 Squadrons RAF.

Flg Off R.L.(later Air Marshal Sir Richard) Atcherley (left) and Flt Lt G.H. (later Wing Commander) Stainforth after winning the 1929 Kings Cup Race in Grebe IIIDC J7520 on 5/6 July 1929. This aircraft was subsequently sold to the Royal New Zealand Air Force.

NZ501, the first of three Grebes for the RNZAF delivered during 1928, seen at Wigram Air Base. None of them had the additional V-struts at the wing tip.

Rebuilt in 1926, Grebe G-EBHA had a Bristol Jupiter IV engine driving the Hele-Shaw constant-speed variable pitch propeller and with Gamecock-style tail unit, upper wing ailerons and landing gear. Here it flies low over Hucclecote Airfield.

J7519, the first of 20 Grebe IIIDC two-seat aircraft pictured at Hucclecote in July 1924, was a trials aircraft for six years before writing itself off while landing at Farnborough.

Opposite, bottom: A Grebe II at Martlesham Heath. The additional V-struts, dubbed 'Folland's Cock's Cradle', support the upper wing overhang to prevent flutter. Note the low-pressure tyres.

Above: Grebe IIIDC 7519 at the A&AEE in May 1925 after anti-flutter struts had been fitted to the wings.

Above: Grebe IIs J7385 and J4000 attached to the rigid airship R-33 before being released after an ascent from Pulham on 21 October 1926.

The pilot goes aboard Grebe NZ502 at Wigram.

A splendid air-to-air photograph of an RNZAF Grebe, NZ502.

An RNZAF Grebe caught in the gunner's camera gun-sights in a Vickers Vildbeeste aircraft during an air display at Rongotai on 4 June 1938.

Officer C. Mackenzie-Richards in the second Grebe had difficulty starting his engine; when it finally fired up he was launched successfully and landed safely at Cardington, Bedfordshire.

Grebe Squadrons

Between 1923 an 1929, six first-line Home Defence squadrons flew Grebes; happily, however, their pilots were never called upon to fire their two guns in anger. The first Grebes to enter RAF service joined 111 Squadron in October 1923 at Duxford, Cambridgeshire, where it had recently reformed. Only one flight was equipped with aircraft from the first batch of twelve Grebes produced. Later a two-seat Grebe MkIIIDC was taken on charge. In March 1924 Biggin Hill-based 56 Squadron had a Grebe for a month's type trials, but it was not until October that 25 Squadron based at Hawkinge in Kent became the first to be fully equipped with Grebes. Other units to similarly equip during September 1924–January 1925 were 56 and 32 Squadrons at Kenley, Sussex, and 19 and 29 Squadrons at Duxford in January 1925. Each squadron and several training units had Grebe two-seaters.

The peace-time life of a Grebe squadron involved every kind of flying training; tactics, aerobatics, formation flying, exercises with other squadrons and, as mentioned earlier, display flying at the annual RAF Pageant at Hendon. Grebe squadrons and units flew every year from 1926 to 1931 in this great exhibition of flying which gave the general public an opportunity to see how some of their taxes were being spent.

This Grebe II with the V struts, J7417, served with 19, 25 and 56 Squadrons and 2 Flying Training School between 1924 and 1930.

Grebe II, J7381 of 29 Squadron. This squadron got its incorrect 'XXX' Roman numeral markings when an RAF Airman was told to paint 'Two exes and then one exe'. He did that. The squadron never corrected it. This Grebe was sold to New Zealand as NZ501.

Two Grebe IIs of 25 Squadron take-off in formation, probably from RAF Duxford, Cambridge, where they were based during 1924-29. They carry the squadron's twin black bar markings.

In 1926 Sir Henry Wigram of Christchurch, New Zealand, bought a Grebe for the New Zealand Permanent Air Force which used it for training fighter pilots. Two years later the NZPAF took delivery of another single-seat Grebe and a two-seat trainer bought by the New Zealand Government which remained in service until the latter part of 1938.

The Gamecock

Clearly, with the Grebe design Henry Folland had still clung to a policy of design evolution at the drawing board and there had been subtle changes in overall appearance. While the S.E.5 and S.E.5a had had a sexy slenderness the Grebe had acquired a more robust muscular air about it created by its stubby radial-engined nose, short fuselage and 29ft wingspan. Further evolution produced his 1925 Gamecock biplane fighter which was a developed and more burly aeroplane.

The Gamecock's design was intended to overcome the several major problems which had plagued the Grebe, whose Jaguar engine had a poor power-to-weight ratio that could burst into flames in the air, was unreliable and was thoroughly unpopular with ground crews. Although the Grebes were loved for their aerobatic handling, wing flutter and poor spin recovery in early production aircraft took their toll of pilots' lives. In the design of its successor the usual internally wire-braced wooden fuselage structure with light wooden formers was beefed-up with several bulkheads. One could see here the influence the stress-man in Howard Preston's make-up had on Folland's design.

Other changes were the use of a mild-steel engine-carrying bulkhead, an aluminium and asbestos fire-proof bulkhead aft of it and the internal mounting of the two Vickers MkI .303in guns in troughs low down on the front fuselage flanks from where they were synchronised

An unidentifiable Gamecock MkI with a Jupiter VI engine, increased area upper ailerons and a horn-balanced rudder.

The third Gamecock MkI, J7757, with a Jupiter VI engine, is seen at the A&AEE for performance trials in September 1925.

to fire between the cylinders and through the propeller disc. Gone was the S.E.5a tail unit; in its place was a larger curved fin and horn-balanced rudder though it kept the ventral fin inherited from the S.E.5. The single-bay wooden wings were sharply staggered, had the H.L.B. section and spanned just less than 30ft. The airframe was fabric-covered except for wooden decking round the cockpit and metal panels round the front fuselage and engine.

Folland certainly made the correct decision when he jettisoned the questionable Jaguar and replaced it with a Bristol 455hp Jupiter MkVI nine-cylinder air-cooled radial engine which was lighter, less complex and much more reliable during tests at Filton, Gloucestershire. In July 1924 these were sufficiently promising to motivate the Air Ministry to issue Specification 37/23 covering a further development of the Grebe powered with the 398hp Jupiter MkIV engine. Ordered the following month, surprisingly as the Grebe MkII, the prototype, J7497, was built in six months with two more aircraft being ordered. By then the new aeroplane was named Gamecock. The first production Gamecock – J7497 and flown by Larry Carter – first got airborne at Hucclecote in February 1925 and was whisked off to Martlesham Heath and the renamed Aeroplane & Armament Experimental Establishment (A&AEE) for fighter performance trials. During these trials experienced RAF pilots were enthusiastic about the general handling of this latest of Folland's fighters. The major complaint that they voiced was that when pulling out of a dive and in a high g-turn the aeroplane 'sank' bodily, even though the elevators were very effective in other flight conditions. Strangely, however, although this new aeroplane was also heir to the Grebe's wing flutter and had its own spinning problems, their initial reports made little or no reference to them! Folland had some lengthy

Flown fast and low in 1927 by Howard Saint, Gloster Aircraft's test pilot, Gamecock MkII, J7910, was converted from a Gamecock MkI. It has parallel ailerons and a larger fin. Note the change of company name.

Howard Saint, accompanied by his dog, sits on a Gamecock's wheel and nonchalantly holds a cigarette while resting between test flights in 1926.

The performance of the company's cleaned-up Gamecock demonstrator, registered G-EBNT in March 1926, was superior to that of the standard Gamecock.

discussions with Larry Carter and the A&AEE pilots, particularly regarding spinning, and sometime in 1927 V-shaped struts were fitted to brace the overhang of the upper wing to combat wing flutter. In the squadrons this modification, which robbed the Gamecock of a substantial number of miles per hour, sadly caused the fighter to be dubbed 'Folland's Cock's Cradle'. Other problems were centred on the normally aspirated Jupiter engine and its pilot-controlled variable timing gear. Two more Gamecocks were ordered for engine trials and by July 50 hours of flying had been logged.

The second Gamecock, J7756, carrying the No.1 marking in the New Types Park at the Hendon RAF Pageant in June 1925 led the fly-past of six of the other new types. At last, in September, with a contract worth £79,500, the Air Ministry ordered thirty Gamecocks to Specification 18/25, powered by Bristol 455hp Jupiter MkVI engines. A further sixty

Left: Gamecock G-EBNT was used for flight trials and demonstrations of the Hele Shaw variable pitch propeller which was being sponsored at Hucclecote by Gloster Aircraft.

Below: With narrow chord ailerons and a centre-section J7910 was one of two Gamecocks used for a series of wing anti-flutter trials by Gloster Aircraft.

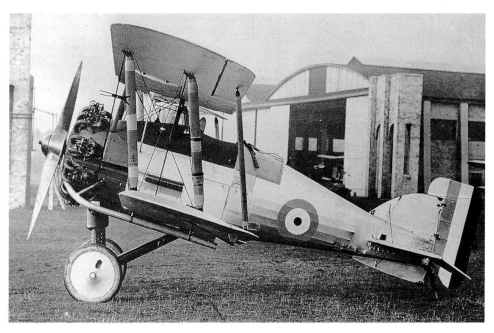

Unofficially named the Gamecock MkIII, J8047 in August 1928, had a lengthened fuselage and a much modified tail unit for spinning trials. It went to a scrap yard in April 1934.

Bought from the scrap yard for £25 by Lincolnshire farmer J.W. Tomkins in May 1934, Gamecock J8047 was rebuilt with a Bristol Bulldog IIA's 490hp Jupiter VIIFP engine. It is seen in the barnyard with Mr Tomkins in the centre of the group.

With its Certificate of Airworthiness issued on 24 September 1935, G-ADIN stands ready for its second 'first flight'. Mr Tomkins flew it to oversee work on several large farms near Apethorpe, Lincolnshire and to seed fields too wet for horses to work.

Left: The horses' ears prick-up as Farmer Tomkins in his Gamecock keeps an eye on their progress with the ploughing.

After a heavy landing G-ADIN turned over and was a complete write-off. Mr Tomkins survived, only to later lose his life in a road accident.

Gamecock MkIs were built in three batches for the RAF plus two, in which Folland had introduced a small centre section on the upper wing and larger rudder, were flown on various trials by the A&AEE and by Farnborough's RAE. Two more were produced as pattern aircraft for Finland, which licence-built fifteen Gamecocks with a lengthened rear fuselage and the small upper-wing centre section.

Gamecock Squadrons

When the first Gamecocks were delivered to 43 Squadron at RAF Henlow, Bedfordshire, in March 1926 they supplemented the three squadrons of Grebes still in RAF service rather than replaced them. Now flying Gamecocks, the squadron took the unofficial name 'The Fighting Cocks' following the Air Ministry's proposal that all squadrons and units should adopt individual badges and accompanying mottoes. In addition, the aircraft carried black-and-white-chequered squadron markings on the wings and fuselage. 43 Squadron flew Gamecocks until June 1928 when it converted to Armstrong Whitworth Siskin MkIIIa fighters.

Meanwhile, also at Henlow, 23 Squadron re-equipped with Gamecocks in April 1926, just a week or two later than 43 Squadron. During September at Kenley, Surrey, 32 Squadron gave up its Grebe MkIIs and received its first Gamecocks. It was not until January 1928 that Gamecocks appeared with 17 Squadron's black double-zig-zag markings at Upavon, Wiltshire; however, eight months later Siskins replaced them. The last to receive Gamecocks was 3 Squadron, which joined 17 Squadron at Upavon in August 1928.

Although Folland's Gamecock was well regarded by the majority of RAF pilots who flew the type, it appeared that neither he nor they were sufficiently skilled to completely

Twelve Gamecock MkIs of 23 Squadron lined-up for inspection with their air and ground crews on a grey, wet day at RAF Kenley in 1927. Four years later the nearest one, J8084, was smashed on the ground by a passing Bulldog!

One of the two pattern Gamecock MkIIs, based on the long-fuselage design, which were bought by the Finnish Government for the Finnish National Aircraft Factory to copy.

This rear view of a Finnish pattern Gamecock shows the centre-section inserted in the upper wing which caused the interplane struts to be splayed out at the top.

A pattern Gamecock on Finnish skis at Lagus in March 1928.

The first Kukko, the Finnish-built Gamecock, minus its fabric covering, on the State Aircraft Factory stand in the First International Air Exhibition in Helsinki in August–September 1929.

This Kukko has modified wing bracing and a cockpit head fairing. Kukkos flew with Finnish Air Force Squadrons 24, 29 and 34 during 1929–35.

An early stage in the construction of an authentic replica Gamecock by the Gloucestershire Aviation Collection and Jet Age Museum. It shows the fuselage and tail unit wire-braced wooden structure, metal landing gear and the restored Jupiter engine.

This close-up view of the Gamecock replica's rear fuselage and tail unit reveals the two vertical three-start square-thread screw jacks to adjust the tailplane's incidence in flight

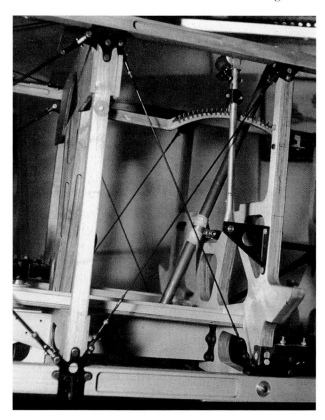

The vertical tube to the right of this picture of the replica's cockpit is the pilot's tailplane-incidence control handle which engages with the toothed quadrant at its top.

uncover the cause of his chubby little fighter's spinning problems or the bodily 'sinking' which manifested itself when diving. Hugh Burroughes, who, it will be remembered, was a founding director of Gloucestershire Aircraft Co., told the author:

> The large unsupported overhang of the outer portion of the upper wing had caused it to flutter and the short fuselage contributed to our spinning problems. These led to a period of modification delays which set us back some five critical years and let our competitors overtake us in the field of fighter aircraft design.

Meanwhile, in Finland, the licence-built Gamecocks, renamed the Kukko, began entering service with three squadrons of the Finnish Air Force in December 1929. One Kukko remained airworthy until September 1944.

The Gorcock

Between 1924 and 1927 Folland, while still heavily involved with the development of the Gamecock, led the design of a series of biplane fighters built only in penny numbers. The first of these was the Gorcock (named after a male red grouse) of which three were built. The last of this trio was a milestone, not only in Henry Folland's career but in the annals of the Gloucestershire Aircraft Co. This was simply because it was Folland and the Company's first military aeroplane to be designed with an all-metal structure.

Although in the general design stages of the Grebe and Gamecock Folland had drawn to some extent on his experience with the Bamel and the Gloster MkI floatplane racer, his design work on the Gorcock helped to pave the way for the company's general adoption of metal for its airframe structures.

In May 1924 Gloucestershire Aircraft Co. received a £24,000 Air Ministry contract for the design and production of three experimental single-seat fighters to Specification 24/23 to be powered by the Napier Lion engine. This was an unusually configured twelve-cylinder, liquid-cooled, broad-arrow in-line engine having three banks of four cylinders. It was a well-tried engine and Folland had used it in the Mars MkI Bamel and in the Gloster MkI and MkII floatplane racers. The first two Gorcocks, which were, in effect, flying test-beds, were designed with a metal fuselage structure and wooden wings; however, the third aircraft was to have an all-metal airframe.

Design work began under Folland's direction in the following month, but its progress was slow because many of the design office staff were still involved with work on the Gamecock and development of the Gloster MkII racer. It was more than a year before the first Gorcock – serialled J7501 – was completed. It resembled the Gamecock MkI in appearance, but the exceptionally neat installation of the 450hp reduction-geared Lion IV engine, the pointed spinner and the manner in which the three cylinder banks were faired into the fuselage gave an overall impression of sleekness that revealed Folland's hand in these design features. However, there appeared to be a retrograde step in that a Grebe-type tail unit was used, but this was soon replaced by the more familiar Gamecock design.

At that time the Air Ministry was examining the relative merits of reduction-geared and direct-drive engines and the Gorcocks were to provide comparative performance figures from these two types. Thus, the second aircraft, serialled J7502, was fitted with a 525hp direct-

J7501, the first Gorcock experimental fighter, had metal fuselage structure, wooden wings and a geared Napier Lion engine. The blister on the fuselage side gave the pilot greater access to the gun. Note the Grebe-style tail unit.

This view of a Gorcock shows the two gravity-fed fuel tanks in the upper wings.

The second Gorcock, J7502, with metal and wood structure, was powered by a direct-drive Lion engine. All three Gorcocks were armed.

The third all-metal Gorcock, J7503, with a geared Lion engine. The 'drum'-shaped radiator between the landing gear legs and narrow-chord ailerons are noteworthy.

drive Lion VIII. Initially, these two wooden-winged aeroplanes were used to test a number of different types of radiators on Lion engines. During the flight-test programme at Hucclecote both Napier and Gloucestershire Aircraft Co. experimental engineers experienced great difficulty in getting all three banks of the Lion's cylinders to fire evenly. Eventually, engine running was undertaken at night so that the colour of the exhaust flame could be checked. Redesigned carburettor air intakes solved the problem, but only after some months' delay. The first two Gorcocks which inaugurally flew in 1925 were delivered to the A&AEE in July and September respectively. It was not until mid-1925 that design of the third Gorcock began and this aeroplane, with a geared Lion IV engine, was not delivered until April 1927. At the A&AEE it recorded a top speed of 174mph, some 30mph faster than the fighters then in RAF squadron service. All three were test flown at Hucclecote and at the A&AEE for different periods between 1925 and 1931. Sadly, the first Gorcock – with wooden wings – broke up during a test flight in September 1929. An unusual feature of the Gorcocks was that despite their research flying role all three fighters carried two Vickers guns with ammunition.

The Guan

Meanwhile, early in 1925, the Air Ministry awarded a £22,500 contract to Gloucestershire Aircraft Co. for three experimental single-seat high-altitude fighters to meet Specification

17/24. Named the Guan (a South American turkey) they were to be specially built to flight-test supercharged aero-engines. Folland intended to combine in one design the Gorcock's high top speed, with a substantial increase in the service ceiling. He achieved his objective.

Inevitably similar to the early Gorcocks in construction, the Guan had an all-metal fuselage structure with wooden wings employing the Gloster H.L.B. combination first used in the Grouse some two years earlier. Like all its predecessors from Folland's drawing board there was no centre section in the upper wings which joined on the aircraft's centre line. The first Guan, serialled J7722, was powered by a Napier 450hp-geared Lion IV equipped with an exhaust-driven turbo-supercharger fitted on the front of the engine below the propeller shaft. This resulted in a great array of external 'plumbing' with long pipes leading exhaust gases forward to energise the supercharger's turbine, the casing of which was connected to the Lion's air intakes. Completed in June 1926, J7722 was delivered to the RAE at Farnborough in August of that year.

In the same month Gloucestershire Aircraft Co. acquired both the design and manufacturing rights to the Hele-Shaw Beacham constant-speed, fixed-pitch and variable-pitch, metal-bladed propellers and was sponsoring their development. Although Folland had used fixed-pitch metal-bladed propellers on two of his earlier racing floatplanes, it is believed that he had not until this juncture used one on any of his fighter aircraft.

By the end of 1926, a year when Folland and Preston were juggling with at least five different designs and projects, Gloucestershire Aircraft Co. had become a well-known name not only in the United Kingdom but also in many other countries – where it was almost unpronounceable. Hugh Burroughes, Folland and other members of the Board had become increasingly aware of the problems associated with this unwieldy title and believed that it should be changed to something more simple. Burroughes told the author, 'Once you leave Dover no one can pronounce Gloucestershire'. Thus, on 11 November

An experimental high-altitude fighter, the Guan was used to test turbo-supercharged and geared Lion engines. Note the external 'plumbing' under the propeller. It is pictured at the RAE Farnborough in September 1926.

1926 Gloucestershire Aircraft officially changed its name to the more easily pronounced and written Gloster Aircraft Company Ltd. (GAC).

The second Guan, serialled J7723, was powered by a 525hp direct-drive Lion VI engine with an exhaust-driven turbo-charger which was more neatly installed on top of the cowling above the propeller shaft. It was completed early in 1927 and was flown to Farnborough on 8 April. During trials the supercharged Lions maintained maximum power output up to 15,000ft, where this Guan had a top speed of 175mph, and pushed its Service Ceiling up to 31.000ft. (Service Ceiling was where an aircraft's rate-of-climb had dropped to 100ft per minute.) However, from a reliability point of view, the superchargers were a constant source of problems. While the Napier company made a number of modifications to these units and the system generally, few of these problems were overcome and the supercharger-development programme was abandoned. Plans to build a third Guan with a 500hp Napier Lioness inverted geared engine that would have been similarly supercharged were also shelved. Before work on this programme was finally brought to an end, the first Guan was flown with Hele-Shaw fixed-pitch and variable-pitch propellers.

The Goldfinch

By the early 1920s Folland – who was increasingly aware of the design limitations of wooden-aircraft structures and was studying all-metal design projects – had been urging the company to make the change to metal airframes. He believed that a bolted-up metal construction with the necessary stiffness could overcome the wing and tail flutter which, it will be remembered, had plagued the Grebe and Gamecock. He was not alone. The Air

The clean lines of the propeller and engine installation, the Gamecock-style fin-and-rudder and the asymmetric centre-section struts are interesting features of J7940, the Goldfinch high-altitude fighter prototype. It marked Gloster's change to metal structures.

Ministry was already seriously considering making metal structures mandatory and only awarding production contracts for designs embodying them. Folland's bold move did not go unnoticed and in January 1926 the Company received a £10,000 Air Ministry contract for an all-metal version of the Gamecock, to meet Specification 16/25 – which was to be named the Goldfinch – for development into a high-altitude fighter.

Despite this order, some of the company's directors who had had a lifetime of woodworking experience, believed that a wholesale change to metal airframes was premature. However, to get things moving, Hugh Burroughes personally bought a half interest in the well-established Steel Wing Company, which had been preaching the benefits of steel in aircraft since 1919. He then moved it to Gloster's factory where Folland and Preston would have the benefit of Steel Wing's design experience alongside them. This investment would prove of great value to GAC.

Apart from its metal structure Folland had embodied a number of new design features in the Goldfinch which had been designed in two distinct forms. One had the external appearance of the Gamecock MkII but had metal wings and tail structures with a mixed wood and metal fuselage. In its revised form the prototype Goldfinch, serialled J7940, had a longer fuselage with a steel primary structure and tail unit similar to that on the Gamecock J8047, which had been unofficially designated the Gamecock MkIII. Among Folland's earlier design studies were a pair of high-tensile steel wing spars. The Gloster Lattice Girder spar had heavy-gauge drawn-steel booms with a light steel strip lattice web which produced a very robust lightweight structure; the other was a box-section spar, similar to a Steel Wing design, described as consisting of high-tensile steel rolled to a 'triple-barrelled shotgun section' boom with a continuous web.

Wings with both types of spars were flown in different combinations in upper and lower wings. Steel predominated in the Goldfinch's fuselage with duralumin in some substructures and aluminium for cowling and fairings. The forward fuselage was an unbraced square steel

This view of the Goldfinch reveals its parallel-chord ailerons, the horn-balanced rudder and Folland's 'trademark' ventral fin.

The different spans and shape of the Goldfinch's wings are very apparent in this photograph. What appear to be two fuel tank vents can be seen on top of the centre-section.

In November 1927 the 'naked' form of the Goldfinch before covering shows the metal fuselage and wooden wings with fuel tanks installed.

tube joined by flat plates bolted through the longerons and struts. The rear fuselage had round tubes with steel tie-rod bracing and joined by bolted steel plates wrapped over the longerons. This structure was given shape by spruce formers and stringers. The pilot could adjust the tailplane in flight. The wide-track landing gear had rubber in compression suspension with oil dashpot shock absorbers. The Goldfinch's Bristol 436hp Jupiter MkV radial engine was supercharged for the high-altitude role, fuel being carried in two gravity feed tanks in the upper wings. However, it is believed that this engine was replaced by a supercharged 450hp Jupiter MkVIIF engine. The standard armament of two fixed forward-firing Vickers .303in machine-guns was carried in troughs in the fuselage sides.

Production of the revised version of the Goldfinch was completed in May 1927 and the aeroplane was delivered to the A&AEE where very satisfactory reports were obtained. A high top speed of 172mph at 10,000ft, 157mph at 20,000ft plus a 27,000ft Service Ceiling were recorded. When Specification F9/26 for a new all-metal day and night fighter for the RAF was issued by the Air Ministry in January, GAC firmly believed that the Goldfinch would be ordered. It was not to be. Sadly, its fuel capacity and military-load capability failed to measure up to requirements and the Bristol Bulldog got the contract. At least its design and manufacture provided GAC with valuable experience in creating metal-structured aircraft.

The Gambet

Again the year 1926 figured large in GAC's history. In that year the Imperial Japanese Navy decided that its Gloucestershire Sparrowhawk fighters, which were only about four years old, needed to be replaced with a more up-to-date aeroplane. In April the

This Gambet naval fighter with a Jupiter VI engine was ignored by the Air Ministry. It was bought by Nakajima Hikoki K.K. in Japan as a pattern aircraft for its A1N1 fighter based on the Gambet.

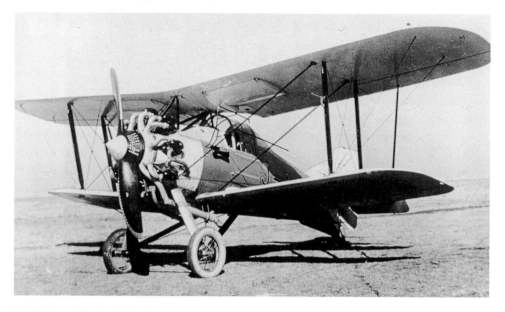

J-AAMB, a civilianised Nakajima A1N1, with an enclosed cockpit and exhaust-collector ring on its Nakajima Jupiter VI engine.

Navy's technical staff instructed three Japanese aircraft manufacturers to submit their proposals for a new series of ship-borne fighters. To boost its chances of securing a contract Nakajima Hikoki K.K. opened discussions with GAC with the intention of acquiring manufacturing rights for the Gamecock and the purchase of a pattern aircraft. Coincidentally, Folland was examining the design of a naval fighter, named the Gambet, which he hoped would be of interest to the Air Ministry and to other naval air arms as a carrier-borne fighter. His hopes were partly realised in 1927 when Nakajima bought a single Gambet as a pattern aircraft as well as a licence to build them in Japan.

Powered by a Bristol 450hp Jupiter MkVI radial engine, structurally and visually the Gambet was very similar to the Gamecock. The fuselage was a wooden structure internally braced by metal rods and the wooden wings were like the Guan. Owing to the fact that a good forward view was necessary for pilots landing on aircraft carriers, the top surface of the front fuselage was markedly sloped down. With the Gamecock's wing flutter in mind, Folland had braced the upper wing's overhang beyond the interplane struts with streamlined wires. The long-stroke landing gear copied that of the Goldfinch but had deck-arrester jaws on the axle casing. Flotation bags were carried in the fuselage and the Gambet had oxygen and night-flying equipment for the pilot. The standard fuselage-mounted two-gun armament was carried with provision for four 20lb bombs on racks under the lower wing.

When flight trials with the unmarked prototype were extremely successful GAC was eager to submit the Gambet for evaluation as a fleet fighter by the A&AEE. Although its performance was superior to that of the existing carrier-borne fighters, the Gambet was completely ignored by the Air Ministry.

With a pattern aircraft and a complete set of drawings in Japan, Nakajima's design team, led by Takao Yoshida, introduced a number of changes to the Gambet, principally to suit local production techniques. In addition the pattern aircraft's original Bristol-built 450hp Jupiter MkVI was replaced by a 520hp Nakajima-built Jupiter MkVI. The Gambet was then test flown against prototypes of the Aichi Tokei Denki K.K. and Mitsubishi Jukogyo K.K. fighters. These two aeroplanes proved to be heavier, less manoeuvrable and no match for the Gambet in a dog-fight. Folland's fighter was an excellent gun-platform and met the Imperial Japanese Navy's requirements.

In April 1929 the Gambet entered production as the Navy Type 3 Carrier Fighter Model 1 or A1N1 (Type 3 indicated the acceptance of the aircraft during the third year of the reign of Emperor Hirohito; A1N1 indicated it was (A) a carrier-borne fighter, (1) the first type accepted by the Navy under its new designation system; (N) built by Nakajima; and (1) the first version. By the end of 1930 a total of fifty A1N1s, all powered with Nakajima Jupiter MkVI engines and carrying a pair of 7.7mm machine guns, had been built. Further development by Nakajima included the fitting of a 520hp Nakajima Kotobuki 2 air-cooled radial engine turning a two-blade metal propeller. In this form the aircraft became the A1N2, of which 100 were built during 1930-32.

A1N1s and A1N2s Squadrons.

These Japanese-built fighters flew with land-based and carrier-based units and were without doubt the best fighter aircraft operated by the Imperial Japanese Navy during the early 1930s. After Japan's invasion of Manchuria in the Autumn of 1931, on 22 February 1932 these Navy fighters were called into action in an engagement over Sochu in China. Navy Captain Nogi Ikuda, flying the third production A1N2, shot down a Boeing 218 fighter flown by a noted US pilot, Robert Short, serving as a flying instructor with the Chinese forces, who had just destroyed two A1N2s. On 26 April A1N2s destroyed a group of enemy aircraft over China to further enhance their formidable reputation in combat. Both variants continued in Imperial Japanese Navy service until withdrawn from operational units in 1935. Numbers of the surviving aircraft were then sold to civilian operators for use as communication aircraft, as trainers after modification to two-seaters and for weather reconnaissance.

The Gnatsnapper

Yet again 1926 was to figure in Folland's design programme. This was Specification N.21/26 for a single-seat deck-landing fighter which was contested by eleven different aircraft. The Gloster entrant was the Gnatsnapper with design work beginning in June 1927. Of conventional all-metal construction, which included the Gloster lattice-type steel spars, an unusual feature was the hinged engine bearers which allowed the engine to be swung to either side for easy access to its rear face.

Problems with the Bristol 450hp Mercury MkII radial engine, which gave up if the throttle was opened rapidly and was some 20 per cent heavier than specified, did not endear it to Gloster pilots and when the Gnatsnapper MkI, N227, was finally delivered to the

The single-bay-winged Gnatsnapper I, N227, had a Jupiter VII engine, two gun armament in side-mounted troughs and large horn-balanced rudder.

N227 as the Gnatsnapper II with an uncowled Jaguar VIII engine, guns mounted in the top of the fuselage and a restyled tail unit.

The partially covered fuselage of the Gnatsnapper II showing its structure, which was typical of Folland's designs, internal equipment and armament.

To provide easy access to the rear face of the Gnatsnapper's Jaguar VIII engine it could be swung to either side as seen here.

N227's cut-away centre-section and lower wing root provided an improved view for the pilot.

Gnatsnapper II flown at low level at Hucclecote by Howard Saint in November 1930.

Gnatsnapper II with a cowled, Jaguar VIII engine.

With two-bay wings and a steam-cooled version of the Rolls-Royce Kestrel, later named Goshawk, the Gnatsnapper II looked remarkably sleek.

The 'new-look' Gnatsnapper II with its Goshawk engine and wing leading-edge condensers.

N254 was the second of the two Gnatsnappers. It had a Mercury IIA engine, a bigger rudder and wing flaps.

A&AEE in May 1929 with a Jupiter MkVII engine and received some good reports, it was too late to join the party! However, because of widespread engine problems a second Ship Fighter Competition was held. With some changes to its tail unit and ailerons and powered by an Armstrong Siddeley 540hp Jaguar MkVIII fourteen-cylinder, twin-row radial engine to become the Gnatsnapper MkII, it was flown again but was badly damaged when it turned over during landing. This finally ended Gloster's hopes for a contract. Nevertheless, N227 was powered with a Rolls-Royce Goshawk, an evaporatively cooled variant of a 525hp Kestrel MkII twelve-cylinder vee geared and supercharged engine employing wing leading-edge condensers. Now designated Gnatsnapper MkIII, it returned to the A&AEE in June 1931 for further trials. Although the Air Ministry was very keen to see this type of power unit in service aircraft, it was believed that its condensers would be very vulnerable to enemy gunfire. N227 was then taken over by Rolls-Royce at Hucknall where it test-flew the 600hp Goshawk MkIII engine before being scrapped in 1934.

The Gauntlet

It is no overstatement to say that the Gloster SS.18 was the first direct forerunner of the Gladiator. Certainly Folland's penchant for design evolution rather than revolution referred to earlier, was apparent in three Gladiator precursors. This was not surprising. They were all based on the same airframe serialled J9125. It served to flight test high-altitude handling and gun firing, the Bristol Mercury MkI installation and cowling and a wide range of streamlining design features. The last of these checks took place during aerodynamic checks in the RAE's 24ft wind tunnel at Farnborough. Unknowingly, all were beneficial to the future Gladiator programme.

During the first decade following the end of the First World War, the performance of most of the RAF's fighter aircraft was marginally sufficient to enable them to cope with that of the bombers taking part in annual exercises. This cosy situation was shattered when, in 1925, the private-venture Fairey Fox light bomber burst upon the scene. Powered by a US-built Curtiss 400hp D.12 vee in-line engine (not by a Fairey licensed-built D.12 named the Felix, as so often reported) and ith its 156mph top speed the Fox put to shame the performance capabilities of the current RAF fighters by out pacing and out climbing them and seriously embarrassing their pilots!

When contemplating a specification for a new high-performance aeroplane to replace the Gamecock a major feature was combating the long-standing wing and tail surface flutter problems. The answer was the mandatory use of metal structures to provide the required stiffness to overcome them. Thus, in April 1926, the Air Ministry produced Specification F9/26. It called for a day and night fighter with all-metal structure but still powered by a radial engine and armed with only two guns. A number of manufacturers prepared designs to meet it; indeed, as the competitive trials eventually continued for many months, several were able to submit more than one design.

Gloster's hopes for the Goldfinch ran high and Folland believed that it would win the F.9/26 contract. Unfortunately, as recorded earlier, this handsome biplane was eliminated in the assessment trials. Then Specification F.20/27 was issued in summer 1927, Bristol's

Gloster's SS.18, J9125, partially painted, stands ready for the photographer in July 1929. The stringers in its fabric-covered rear fuselage, the side gun trough and the tail skid are clearly visible.

J9125 on a test flight at Hucclecote on a misty morning in 1929. Surprisingly, Folland used two-bay wings for this high performance fighter.

Redesignated the SS.19 Multi-gun fighter, J9125 carries six guns and has a cowled Jupiter VIIF engine.

With four wing guns removed, but with wheel fairings, a Jupiter VIIF engine and a restyled tail unit, J9125 became the SS.19A.

Gloster's chief inspector, 'Dogshead' Green, and his wife, accompanied Henry Folland and his pipe when he attended the 24 June 1933 RAF Hendon Display where the SS.19B flew in spite of bad weather.

Now powered by a Mercury VIS engine J9125 became the SS.18B.

This close-up view of the SS.19B's landing gear shows the very high standard of workmanship in its struts and slender wheel fairings.

Bulldog won the order. However, its performance was only marginally superior to that of the new Gloster SS.18 and Folland pressed ahead with its further development.

Powered by the widely criticised Bristol Mercury MkIIA radial engine, which was incapable of delivering anything approaching the promised 500hp, Howard Saint first flew the prototype in January 1929. With a 490hp Bristol Jupiter MkVII engine fitted five months later, J9125 was designated the SS.18A. Full manufacturers' trials resulted in the adoption of a 560hp Armstrong Siddeley Panther MkIII fourteen-cylinder, two-row radial engine and the aircraft was redesignated the SS.18B. Although this produced a 205mph top speed at 10,000ft, the Panther weighed some 220lb more than the Jupiter. Folland again switched engines, going back to a Jupiter MkVIIF with which J9125 became the SS.19 during the summer of 1930. Later, four wing-mounted guns were added to the standard two fuselage guns to temporarily produce the multi-gun variant. It is recorded that one high-ranking RAF officer considered this heavy armament was an unfair advantage for aerial warfare with words like 'unsporting' being bandied about! Then, in 1931, with other airframe refinements, J9125 became the SS.19A. When the reliable 536hp Bristol Mercury VIS was installed in February 1933, J9125 finally became the SS.19B. It would undergo many more changes and designations until September 1933 when Gloster received a production Specification 24/33 and an order for twenty-four aircraft, based on the SS18B with a 645hp Mercury VIS engine and named Gauntlet MkI.

J9125 as the Gauntlet prototype in the 24ft wind tunnel at the Royal Aircraft Establishment at Farnborough in March 1935.

The Gauntlet's airframe was a conventional all-metal structure with fabric covering on the wings and rear fuselage and metal panels on the front fuselage from its nose back to the cockpit. It had a wide-track landing gear with Dowty oleo legs and with differential wheel brakes operated through pedals on the rudder bar. There were some raised eyebrows in RAF Messes at Folland's use of two-bay wings. He was still haunted by memories of the Grebe's and Gamecocks' wing flutter problems and believed this wing design would prevent it in the Gauntlet. Despite the two-bay wings, fixed landing gear and open cockpit the Gauntlet's 230mph top speed and ability to climb to 33,200ft were a tribute to Folland's attention to drag-reducing features. He fitted the structure and equipment into a streamlined fuselage, used thin wing sections with careful design of the wing-to-fuselage and the strut-to-wing joints, rigged them with streamlined bracing wires with all their fittings submerged within the wing and gave meticulous attention to all fittings.

Then, in June 1934, Gloster Aircraft was taken over by Hawker Aircraft Ltd with promises of future big subcontract business for the Hucclecote factory which had not built any of its own-design aircraft since 1928. But back to the Gauntlet: Gerry Sayer, Gloster's chief test pilot, flew the first production Gauntlet MkI, K4081, on 17 December 1934. During the ensuing months several early production Gauntlets were flown at the A&AEE and by 19 Squadron at RAF Duxford, Cambridgeshire.

The Henry Folland/Gloster way of designing and building aeroplanes differed from the Sydney Camm/Hawker method and while this first batch of Gauntlets was produced by Gloster design and manufacturing procedures the following 204 aircraft, designated Gauntlet MkII, embodied Hawker structures. These mainly involved the use of Warren

Girder side panels in the rear fuselage, requiring fewer internal wire bracings, and re-styled wing spars. In addition, the Gauntlet MkII had pneumatically powered flaps on all four wings and the Watts wooden two-blade propellers were replaced by Fairey-Reed fixed-pitch, three-blade metal propellers.

Hucclecote was not the only site producing Gauntlets. In October 1934 the Danish Government obtained a licence to build them in Denmark, paying Gloster £3,750. An uncovered pattern airframe minus engine and armament cost another £2,700. Seventeen Gauntlets, designated Il Js were built by Danish Army Air Service Workshops in Copenhagen serialled J-22 to J-38. The pattern aircraft flew in April 1936, the first two Danish-built aircraft were completed in September, fourteen aircraft appeared during 1937 and the last one flew in January 1938.

Gauntlet Squadrons in Peace & War

In May 1935 when 19 Squadron became the first to receive Gauntlet MkIs, it marked the end of the RAF's open-cockpit biplane-fighter era which had begun in the First World War. Despite some early dismay at its two-bay wings, when Gauntlets began entering other squadrons to replace Bristol Bulldogs, their pilots soon realised that Folland's latest fighter was quite a hot-rod. Not only was it the fastest fighter in the RAF with a 230mph top speed and had the highest service ceiling, it was also a superb aerobatic aeroplane. 19 Squadron, already renowned for its adventurous flying, took full advantage of these features. On 27 June 1936 at the Hendon Display three of its pilots, Flying Officer J.R. MacLachlan and Pilot Officer B.G. Morris led by Flight Lieutenant H. Broadhurst flew their Gauntlets in a tied-together formation aerobatic sequence to delight the thousands of the public present. 19 Squadron retained its Gauntlets until August 1938 when it became the first squadron to receive Spitfires.

It was May 1936 before 56 Squadron got Gauntlet MkIIs at RAF North Weald with 32, 65 and 66 Squadrons receiving theirs in July. This was an era when, with the founding of Fighter Command in the same month, the RAF was regarded by its pilots as 'the world's best flying club'. Seventeen RAF squadrons were re-equipped with Gauntlet MkIIs during the next seven months with five Auxiliary Air Force squadrons getting theirs between November 1938 and January 1939. All took part in Air Exercises, practiced combat tactics, rehearsed aerobatic displays and participated in gunnery and aerobatic competitions.

Had war with Germany come in September 1938 it is still frightening to recall that nearly half of Fighter Command's single-seat fighter force was composed of nine squadrons of Gauntlets with open cockpits and two guns apiece. In the Order of Battle they were supported by seven Gladiator squadrons, two squadrons of Furies and only three Hurricane squadrons. By 3 September 1939 when war came, ten ex-Gauntlet squadrons had converted to Hurricanes and seven had Spitfires.

Some thirty Gauntlets ended their service life with eight UK-based meteorological flights, making daily climbs to high altitudes in all weather conditions. The last record of Gauntlets on RAF strength was on 1 May 1943 when, due to a lack of Gladiators, four Gauntlets joined 1414 Met Flight at Eastleigh, Nairobi for training duties.

Gauntlet MkII, K5296, with 56 Squadron's markings, later flew with 17 Squadron between 1936–39 before becoming a ground instructional airframe 2130M in early 1940.

Gauntlet MkIIs of 56 Squadron fly an impressive five-abreast formation in bright sunshine. K5296 is the aircraft in the middle position.

RAF Gauntlet squadrons were based in Ramleh, Palestine, supporting land forces and in Mersah Matruh and Helwan in Egypt to supplement Gladiator squadrons. When Italy entered the war in June 1940, Gauntlets took part in several fighter-bomber operations in East Africa with an Italian Caproni bomber falling to a Gauntlet's guns. Ex-RAF Gauntlets flown by a Royal Australian Air Force (RAAF) squadron saw action in the Western Desert during December 1940. Meanwhile, in Denmark its seventeen Gauntlets were equipping 1 Eskadrille at Vaerlose near Copenhagen. However, five were lost in accidents and one during a German air attack on Vaerlose. Following Soviet Russia's attack on Finland in November 1939, Great Britain shipped twenty-five ex-RAF Gauntlet MkIIs as aid to Finland to join thirty ex-RAF Gladiators already there. These were deployed to defend southern Finland.

Flying the Gauntlet

In one of his enthralling *Wings of the Weird and Wonderful* books, Captain Eric Brown, RN, who has flown more different types of aircraft than any other pilot in the world, recalls his memories of flying a Gloster Gauntlet:

> Ever since I had seen a marvellous aerobatic display with three Gauntlets of 19 Squadron tied together it had been my dream to fly a Gauntlet. That dream took two years to fulfil and it turned out to be superb. The version I flew was fitted with a Fairey three-blade fixed-pitch metal propeller which gave it a lively take-off and a fair amount of swing to be counteracted. The climb angle was steep and so deliciously simple to execute – just pull back on the stick.

K7810 flew as a target aircraft at Farnborough during early radar trials. It was written off at RAF Wittering after a ground collision with another 213 Squadron Gauntlet.

This ex-Finnish Air Force Gauntlet carries the very appropriate civil registration OH-XGT on its fin. With an Alvis Leonides radial engine replacing its Bristol Mercury it is seen flying again.

No undercarriage or flaps to raise, no propeller pitch to change, no hood to close. However, one had to admit that the Gauntlet, like all the great biplane fighters had poor forward view in anything but cruising diving flight.

My primary aim was, however, to turn this joyous aeroplane inside-out in aerobatics and the sensitivity of its controls made light of loops, rolls, spins and flick manoeuvres. Then, too, there was the exhilaration of being in an open cockpit which makes one more aware of the skid than any instrument and also gives that extra zest to inverted flight. Perhaps the most glorious thing about an open cockpit is it allows the pilot to hear the singing of the bracing wires so that changes of speed in aerobatics become orchestrated. Landing the Gauntlet was, perhaps, a little harder than flying it in any other manoeuvre – but that is a relative statement.

The aircraft handled beautifully in an engine-off glide at 65mph and could be side slipped to within feet of the ground with absolute confidence of precise recovery: in fact, I used to deliberately approach high, not just to side slip off the excess height for the hell of it but to improve the rather mediocre forward view in the glide. All that was required to achieve a three-point landing was a firm backward pressure on the stick at hold-off. However, on touchdown the forward view vanished and one had to lean well to one side of the cockpit to ensure running straight.

The Gauntlet was, of course, not a circus stunt plane but a military fighter and in that respect it was a very good gun platform, although with only two fixed .303in machine guns the fire-power was not heavy.

To sum up, therefore, the Gloster Gauntlet was the forerunner of the high-performance biplane fighters which in turn pointed the way to the high-speed monoplane of the 1930s. It was a memorable aeroplane, beloved by all who were privileged to fly it and it carved a niche for itself in British aircraft design history. It will certainly be remembered as an aerobatic gem.

SEVEN

SPECIFICATION F.7/30
AND THE CONTENDERS

As related earlier, back in 1926 the Fairey Fox light bomber had burst upon the British military aviation scene and, in the hands of 12 Squadron, put to shame the performance capabilities of contemporary RAF fighters by out-pacing and out-climbing them. The Fox's capabilities caused radically new thinking by the Air Council and Air Ministry about air defence requirements in general, the need for a new generation of single-seat fighters in particular and, ultimately, the issue of Specification F.7/30. This was an Air Ministry missive which would be simultaneously welcomed, criticised, highly praised or ignored by various elements of Britain's aircraft industry. Following its issue it was the frequent subject of numerous amendments, but its basic demands remained intact.

Specification F.7/30 was aimed at creating a single-seat fighter with a performance far in advance of contemporary types and the ability to meet on equal – or better – terms any hostile airborne threat to the British Isles. Its importance could not have been too highly rated. Here follows some interesting and important extracts from a 1931 Specification F.7/30.

Dated 1/10/31 a Confidential letter, Ref. No. 17128/30/R.D.A.S., from the Air Ministry's Directorate of Technical Development and signed by its Director, Air Commodore H.M. Cave, accompanied every copy of Specification F.7/30 for a Single-seater day-and-night fighter which was distributed to a selected group of British aircraft manufacturers. It carried a warning paragraph:

> This document is intended for the use of the recipient only and may be used only in connection with work carried out for or on behalf of HM Government. The unauthorised retention or destruction of this document or the disclosure of its contents to any unauthorised person, is forbidden.

This document revealed the innermost thoughts of the Air Council and Air Ministry about a major element of Britain's future air defences and its requirements. Without doubt it was the most adventurous of any produced by the Directorate between the two world wars. The above warning paragraph was, therefore, of prime importance.

The general requirements were set out on page 1 paragraph 1(a):

The configuration of the Blackburn F.3 gave its pilot an unobstructed all-round view upwards but very little below. The short stumpy fuselage sits on the Goshawk engine's heat dissipater.

Bristol Aeroplane's Type 123 with a Goshawk engine had a thin upper wing and a thicker cantilevered lower wing. Note the large landing gear 'trousers' and nose-mounted guns.

The Bristol Type 133 inverted gull-winged monoplane, had a retractable landing gear and a conventional air-cooled Bristol Mercury engine.

The Main Requirements for the Aircraft are:

(i)   Highest possible rate of climb.
(ii)   Highest possible speed at 15,000ft.
(iii)   Fighting view.
(iv)   Manoeuvrability.
(v)   Capability of easy and rapid production in quantity.
(vi)   Ease of Maintenance.

More detailed requirements were set out in paragraphs 1(b) to (h). and on subsequent pages. Designers had the choice of a monoplane or biplane configuration. From today's viewpoint it appears strange that three other acceptable configurations were listed in a paragraph about engine-cooling systems in an early issue of this specification. They were: (i) Aircraft (tractor or pusher) fitted with one or more steam-cooled engines; (ii) Tractor aircraft fitted with two or more water-cooled engines; (iii) Pusher aircraft fitted with two or more water-cooled engines. It had to be suitable for day or night operations and, initially, to have a horizontal speed of not less than 195mph at 15,000ft and a 50mph landing speed with night operations in mind. A metal primary structure was mandatory. In addition, this specification called for an eight-minute climb to 15,000ft and a 28,000ft ceiling which were superior to those of aircraft currently in squadron service, together with a low-wing loading plus good all-round vision for the pilot and no exhaust glare when operating at night. In addition, an oxygen system and two-way radio were to be installed.

The Goshawk-powered Hawker PV.3 was described as 'a pumped-up Fury with Hart wings', but it lacked their sleek lines.

Ultimately this fighter was required to have a level top speed of at least 250mph and, with night operations in mind, a landing speed of not more than 50mph. Armament was to be at least four forward-firing Vickers .303in machine guns with 2,000 rounds of ammunition. However, the wisdom of choosing Vickers guns was questionable; they were very prone to stoppages. Their breeches needed to be accessible in flight so that, in the event of a stoppage, it is said that the pilot would whack the breech with a mallet to free it!

At that time the Air Ministry was having a 'love-affair' with an evaporatively cooled version of the Rolls-Royce Kestrel engine which became the Goshawk. This cooling system was lighter than a traditional liquid-cooling system; moreover, condensing the steam released thirty times more heat than cooling the same flow of water.

While not mandatory, as noted above, Specification F.7/30, page 6, Section 2, sub-paragraph (C) (f) (i) gives priority to: 'aircraft (tractor or pusher) fitted with one or more steam-cooled engines'. Unfortunately, Rolls-Royce discovered that this engine's development was proving more difficult and protracted than had been envisaged. It was a complicated cooling system which invariably spurted steam and boiling water at joints and often failed to work in inverted flight when the steam and water changed places, which was not a good idea. Some designers made provision to protect the pilot from being scalded, others arranged for the 'heat dissipaters' to form part of the aircraft's wing surface, a vulnerable location. Nevertheless, with the promise of large production contracts for the chosen design, the aircraft industry responded to the challenge, but in different ways, with at least six submissions.

Westland F.4's Goshawk was buried in the fuselage and drove the propeller through a long shaft. Note the nose-mounted guns, enclosed cockpit and wheel fairings.

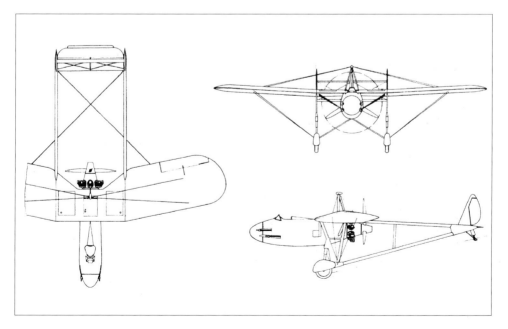

One of two Bristol Aeroplane Company's F.7/30 projects was this ungainly twin-boomed Type 129 with a Mercury IV pusher engine.

Supermarine's Type 224 had 46ft span wings in a fruitless attempt to obtain the specified 50mph landing speed; moreover, the landing gear 'trousers' contributed to its inadequate top speed.

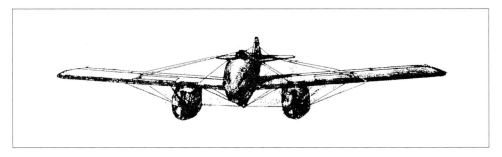

A sketch of Boulton & Paul's P.67 project to F .7/30. Heavily wire-braced, the rectangular plan-form wings carried underslung Napier Dagger engines.

Blackburn, Supermarine and Westland were given Air Ministry prototype contracts and all three embodied the Goshawk MkI in their designs. Hawker's private venture submission also had the Goshawk and Bristol backed its private venture, offering both a Goshawk-powered biplane and a monoplane with one of its own radial engines. In addition it offered the prototype Bulldog IVA with a 640hp Mercury VIS2. Their deadline was September 1933, when preliminary evaluation trials were programmed. and by which time it was anticipated that Rolls-Royce would have produced a fully developed Goshawk.

However, none of the six Specification F.7/30 prototypes met all of the stated requirements and were, in many ways, compromise designs. In addition, because of late delivery of the Goshawks, none of these aircraft were completed by the stipulated date in 1933 and evaluation trials were postponed until 1934.

Ultimately, the Goshawk MkI in George Petty's strangely configured Blackburn F.3 was overheating and the rear fuselage was structurally weak with cracks appearing after preliminary taxiing in July 1934. The Air Ministry was not amused, further work was abandoned. It is believed it never flew, but ended up grounded at RAF Halton's

Electrical and Wireless school. Although the Goshawk appeared to behave itself in Frank Barnwell's Bristol-Type 123 biplane it had incurable lateral instability at high speeds and it was abandoned. The Type 133 monoplane, which Roy (later Sir Roy) Fedden – the dynamic head of Bristol's Engine Division had persuaded Barnwell to design with one of his engines – crashed when its pilot forgot to retract the landing gear before spinning it and he was forced to bale out. Bristol also offered the prototype Bulldog IVA with a 620hp Mercury MkIVSA engine but it was too slow for serious consideration. Influenced by Specification F.7/30. Hawker's high-speed Fury certainly met the speed requirement but as it did not use a Goshawk and had only two guns, it was not submitted. With time slipping away, Sydney Camm created the P.V.3 by designing a scaled-up Fury with smaller Hart wings, the upper one with leading edge condensers for the evaporatively cooled Goshawk engine. When Camm decided to replace it with a liquid-cooled Goshawk MkI it arrived too late and the P.V.3 was withdrawn. Designed by Arthur Davenport, Westland's F.4 biplane had its Goshawk mounted midway along the fuselage, but its top speed was 60mph below the required figure and its fuselage fabric caught fire when Harald Penrose rolled it. The maximum speed of Reginald Mitchell's Supermarine Type 224 monoplane, unofficially named the Spitfire, was too low and its landing speed, even with a 46ft wing span, was too high. In addition to these aircraft several companies had projects which never left the drawing board: John D. North at Boulton and Paul had drafted a twin-engined monoplane, Bristol's projects included a little low-winged monoplane and a twin-boomed pusher-engined design and Westland had reached the wind-tunnel model stage for a Lysander-like parasol-winged monoplane. Undoubtedly it was the failure of these prototypes – for many different reasons – and the on-going successful development of the Gauntlet that further energised Folland's train of thought leading to the Gladiator.

EIGHT

ENTRY OF THE GLADIATORS

It may appear surprising that during the early 1930s Gloster was not among the companies competing for the Specification F.7/30 contract. The reason was that Folland had been too busy with piece-meal private-venture development of the Gauntlet. By 1934, however, it was showing a clean pair of heels to the Fury in the matter of top speed and climb. Thus, with Gloster's directors' unwavering confidence in Folland's capabilities they urged him to concentrate on making major changes to the production Gauntlet to create a new private-venture high-performance fighter to meet the F.7/30 requirements. This was a bold decision as Gloster's financial position was weak.

Drawing on his experience in designing a number of biplane floatplane racers for the Schneider Trophy contests, Folland was ever eager to minimise drag. Thus, he began by throwing away two pairs of the Gauntlet's interplane struts and went for single-bay wings. With them went yards of bracing wires and fittings. To provide strength and rigidity in the single-bay wings he introduced slightly heavier and thicker-gauge wing spars. Next to go were the four landing-gear struts, their bracing wires and axle spreader bar. These were replaced by two rigid streamlined cantilever legs. This type of landing gear was made possible by using the slim Dowty internally sprung wheels which housed the suspension and braking. This wheel was designed in 1930 by George Dowty who – in January 1931 whilst still a member of Folland's design office – formed his own spare-time company, Aircraft Components. Six months later, when Gloster wanted too much money for the sub-contract manufacture of six internally sprung wheels for Japan's Kawasaki company, Dowty quit his Gloster drawing board and, with the help of two friends, made them himself in a Cheltenham garden shed. With these changes it was anticipated that the top speed of the new Gloster fighter would be increased by 15 to 20mph. In addition, at Filton, just thirty miles from Gloster's Hucclecote factory down the A38 main road, the Bristol Mercury ME.30 air-cooled radial engine was delivering some 700hp.

While Folland was confidently forecasting a 250mph top speed for this new private-venture aeroplane, designated the SS.37, he realised that its armament of two fuselage-mounted Vickers Mk III guns synchronised to fire through the propeller disc would not meet Specification F.7/30 requirements. He was worried that with the extra weight and drag of two more guns and ammunition, the magic 250mph would not be attainable. However, in February 1934, Roy Fedden at Bristol, assured Folland that the 800hp

As originally built with a Gauntlet fuselage, engine cowling and open cockpit, the SS.37 prototype is very near the definitive Gladiator in appearance.

Mercury ME.35 would be available by the time that Gloster's new SS.37 could be put into production. This solved the four-gun armament problem and, with the other six types out of the running, it made the SS.37 a viable private-venture contender which would fully meet Specification F.7/30 requirements. But time was of the essence.

It was now becoming clear that the new Supermarine and Hawker single-seat eight-gun monoplane fighters being built would not be in RAF squadrons before the end of 1937 and that some of these units were still equipped with 220mph Furies and others with Bulldogs – which could just make it to 178mph on a good day. There was a great need for an interim fighter to bridge the gap until the monoplanes would arrive. At once Folland and Gloster's directors submitted the SS.37 to the Air Ministry.

In order to get a prototype SS.37 into the air as soon as possible a Gauntlet fuselage with minimum changes was used as the basis. The all-metal fuselage structure was built in three sections; the front one comprised the engine mounting attached to the four longerons; the mid-section housed the fuel and oil tanks and the cockpit while the rear section carried the tail unit. All these sections had Gloster plate-type joints and were internally wire-braced. Light metal formers and stringers provided external shape. Forward of the cockpit the fuselage was clad with removable metal panels with fabric covering the remainder. Among the alterations were those to the upper longerons' front ends to accommodate a large oil cooler curved to match the fuselage shape, and minor reconstruction of an area just behind the open cockpit where a streamlined pilot's headrest was located. Modifications also were made to the lower front fuselage where the cantilever undercarriage legs were attached. The Gauntlet tail unit and spatted tailwheel were retained. The fabric-covered single-bay lower wings were carried on tubular members passing through the fuselage below the bottom longerons while the upper wings were attached to a small centre section carried on four wire-braced struts. Frise ailerons and metal-clad flaps were mounted on all four wings. The Gauntlet's two fuselage-mounted Vickers guns were retained with one Lewis gun carried under each lower wing.

Although a 645hp Mercury VIS engine had been earmarked for this aeroplane, due to some last minute snags at Bristol a lower-powered 530hp Mercury MkIV with a Gauntlet cowling was fitted for the first flight. This came on 12 September 1934, the pilot being P.E.G. 'Gerry' Sayer, Gloster's chief test pilot, who had moved from Hawker Aircraft following that company's acquisition of Gloster Aircraft the previous May. Gloster's airfield and factory occupied land in both the adjoining Brockworth and Hucclecote parishes. When Gloster had moved in from Cheltenham during 1925–28 it chose Hucclecote as its address because it had two daily postal deliveries while Brockworth had only one!

Initially, the SS.37's top speed was only 236mph, but on 28 October 1934 – with a Mercury VIS fitted – 242mph was clocked at 11,500ft. Some more minor modifications were made during flight trials at Hucclecote and on 3 April 1935 this private-venture aeroplane to meet Specification F.7/30 was transferred to Air Ministry charge and serialled K5200. Almost immediately it was attached to 1 Squadron RAF at Tangmere for initial service trials. At the A&AEE, where some eighty flying hours were logged, the SS.37's performance was reckoned to be much better than any achieved by the previous failed F.7/30 entrants. In the following month Gloster submitted details of an improved

The SS.37 shows off its low-powered Mercury engine, fuselage and underwing guns and early design dished wheel discs.

version with the more powerful 830hp Mercury MkIX engine, an enclosed cockpit with sliding canopy, revised tail unit and embodying Hawker-type construction. A 252mph maximum speed at 14,000ft coupled with a 48mph landing speed instantly grabbed the Air Ministry's full attention.

No doubt urged on by the RAF's expansion schemes, the formalities were rushed through in less than two weeks, a production Specification F.14/35 was created and twenty-three aircraft were ordered under contract No.419392/36. It stipulated that all components should be produced before final assembly began. On 29 June 1935, K5200 was flown by an A&AEE pilot in the RAF display at Hendon carrying the New Type Park No.1 marking. Two days later at Hendon, it was s flown by Gerry Sayer in the fourth Society of British Aircraft Constructors' Show. With a great sense of timing, the Air Ministry named this new RAF fighter on the same day. It was the Gladiator.

Development and Flight Testing

With its two days of public 'skylarking' completed, K5200 returned to Hucclecote and, with Air Ministry collaboration, Folland and Preston got started on a programme of modifications to bring it up to near-production Gladiator standard. An 830hp Mercury MkIX engine with a Watts wooden propeller of coarser pitch replaced the earlier Mercury and the fuselage around the cockpit was modified to carry the sliding canopy, which was operated with a chain and sprocket gear. This involved the removal of stringers and building tripods on the upper longerons to carry Hawker-type stringers to form the canopy's rear fairing, into which a radio mast was fitted. Of major importance was the armament to be carried. Because of the problems with the Vickers gun referred to earlier, the Air Ministry examined a number of British and foreign guns to find one which would not need the mallet-bashing treatment. A licence to manufacture the US-built Colt .300in calibre gun was negotiated and its production by Birmingham Small Arms – with .303in calibre and named the Browning gun – was planned. On firing trials it was claimed that the Vickers gun was 600 times more likely to jam than the Browning! Provision was made for this gun to be fitted in later-production Gladiators when they became available. The modern Gladiator would have more than one *gladius*.

Flight testing of the modified and updated K5200 began at Hucclecote in September 1935; by then a second production batch of 180 Gladiator MkIs had been ordered. The Air Ministry also instructed Gloster to complete deliveries to RAF squadrons by the end of 1937. For these renewed flight trials the Air Ministry decided that a Fairey-Reed three-blade fixed-pitch metal propeller was to be fitted in place of the big Watts wooden type. On 23 October 1935 this prototype, powered by a Mercury MkIX engine having the standard .5:1 ratio reduction gear, returned to the A&AEE for comparative trials with different propellers. Unfortunately, the port undercarriage leg collapsed as it landed when the cantilever fulcrum pin on the longeron sheared off. A concerted effort by Gloster and A&AEE engineers quickly completed the repairs to the fuselage and lower wing. There followed some lengthy and searching propeller trials which provoked comments that the three-blade metal propeller had little to offer over the two-blade wooden type.

An early air-to-air photograph of the SS.37 now serialled K5200 for official trials at the A&AEE Martlesham Heath.

Gerry Sayer, Gloster's chief test pilot, positions K5200 for the photographer. Note the positions of the ailerons and elevators in this banked turn and the RAF Hendon Pageant's New Type Park numeral 1 on the nose.

This Gladiator's non-standard cockpit at least has the 'standard six' instrument blind-flying panel. Note the rudder bar and heel slides. The control column handle incorporates the gun-firing button and brake lever.

Close-up view of the Gladiator's landing gear with its streamlined cantilever legs and Dowty internally sprung wheels with new style discs.

The A&AEE's Interim Report M/666B/Int. of September 1937 described comparative tests of Gladiator MkI, K7964, fitted with a 10ft 6in diameter Fairey Reed metal propeller on a Mercury MkIX delivering 840hp at 14,000ft and with a .572:1 ratio reduction gear, against K5200 flying with a standard Mercury MkIX having its normal .5:1 ratio reduction gear. The object of this particular test was to achieve smoother running of this engine. With the metal propeller K5200 notched up 253mph at 14,500ft and the engine performed satisfactorily at 32,000ft. With the Watts two-blader the top speed was 248mph at 14,600ft. K7964 managed only 245mph at 14,200ft. As a result of these and other trials on a third Gladiator MkI it was calculated that although the Watts was lighter and produced a shorter take-off run, it couldn't match the 253mph top speed with the metal-bladed propeller. Thus the metal unit with the .572:1 gear ratio was finally declared the better partnership.

Between 3 April 1935 – when K5200 was taken on Air Ministry charge – and 12 November 1942 when it was struck off charge having logged 473 flying hours, it had shuttled between Hucclecote and the A&AEE, the RAE, Bristol Aeroplane Company and several squadrons and units. K5200 also flew in the 1935 and 1936 SBAC displays at Hendon.

Gladiator MkI

While the production Gladiator was the RAF's last biplane fighter it was also the first to have an enclosed cockpit and to be armed with a battery of four fixed forward-firing guns. Its structure, however, was a well-established design being all-metal and mainly fabric-covered.

The fuselage was built in four numbered sections: No.1 the engine mounting, No.2 front fuselage, No.3 rear fuselage and No.4 tail section. Following Hawker's acquisition of the Gloster company in 1934, Hawker-type structure was used in place of the Gloster design. The side members of each section were Warren girders built up with aluminium and steel tube swaged to a square section at their ends and secured by bolted fishplates. Top and bottom lateral ball-ended steel tubes, which butted into cupped bolts in the fish plates, joined the two side members to complete the 'box' which was internally braced and rigged with adjustable cross wires. Light alloy-notched formers were attached to these fuselage section structures to support light-alloy stringers and give the external shape. The front two sections were clad with metal panels and the remainder of the airframe including control surfaces, but not the flaps which were all-metal, was fabric-covered. The fabric was attached by the patented Gloster wired-on system.

The engine, which turned a 10ft 9in diameter Watts wooden two-blade propeller, was attached by eight bolts to a hexagonal plate which had a fireproof bulkhead on its rear face. Immediately behind this engine mounting was the main undercarriage. It comprised two rigid cantilever tubular members with stub axles, which were carried on the front of the fuselage structure in an A-frame configuration. These axles carried Dowty internally sprung wheels with aerodynamically shaped tyres; the pneumatic brakes were activated by a lever on the control column's spade grip with differential braking by the rudder bar. Aft of the fireproof bulkhead a 20-gallon gravity fuel tank was carried on the top longerons with a 63-gallon main tank below it from which fuel was pumped to the engine via a filter and fuel cock. Oil was contained in a 5-gallon tank under the starboard surface with

Four ailerons, a spatted tailwheel and the pilot's headrest fairing are features of this view of the SS.37.

K6131, the third production Gladiator, climbs steeply over Hucclecote. Delivered to 72 Squadron at RAF Tangmere in March 1937, it was struck off charge in July 1938.

K6131 in straight and level flight in the sunshine.

K6143, an unarmed Gladiator MkI with meteorological equipment on the interplane struts, reveals its large-area curved surface oil cooler on the front fuselage top.

Some 30 Dowty internally sprung wheels ready for delivery to Gloster's factory for the first batch of production Gladiator Is in September 1936.

a large contoured cooler mounted externally above it. Aft of this was the cockpit. A belt-fed gun was carried in an external mild-steel trough on each side of this fuselage section with its 600 round ammunition box inside. An interrupter system ensured that the guns fired a round only when the propeller blades were not in the line of fire. Another gun-related design feature was described by one eminent aviation writer, who noted: 'A subtle touch was evident in the engine cowling, the nose exhaust-collector ring necessitating two exquisitely fashioned scallops, or dimples, in the way of the gun troughs'.

The rear fuselage housed the HF radio and some electrical system equipment while the tail section supported the tail unit which had several unusual design features. The variable incidence tailplane was built up around two tubular spars and fabricated light-alloy ribs, the elevator being hinged to the rearmost spar. The tailplane was activated through a cockpit hand wheel which operated a duplicated cable and chain-and-sprocket system. The fin had a similar structure with the bottom section of its vertical tubular spar fitting neatly down into the fuselage tail section's tubular sternpost and being bolted to it. The rudder, which had a slightly different shape from that on the prototype, was hinged on both these tubular members. Both the elevator and rudder control surfaces were operated by the pilot's conventional control column and rudder bar through duplicated cables. The fuselage tail section also carried the fixed castoring and self-centring Dowty tailwheel.

The straight, sharply staggered wings had two Hawker-type spars in which the steel top and bottom booms were of a rolled, eight-sided section with a corrugated plate web having strong points where the four interplane struts were attached. This wing-structure was completed by fabricated light alloy ribs, stringers and drag struts. In the lower wing the spars were attached to two tubular members in the front fuselage section. The upper wings were attached to a wide-span centre section, which had leading and trailing edge cut-outs to improve the pilot's field of vision, and was carried on two pairs of wire-braced struts. Frise ailerons were carried on both wings, the upper ones being activated through duplicated wires attached to the lower ones that were operated through a cable, push rod and chain-and-sprocket system. Hydraulically operated metal-clad split-trailing-edge flaps were also fitted to the inboard ends of the upper and lower wings and were controlled by a small lever on the port side of the cockpit.

Records show that the first production batch of twenty-three Gladiator MkIs had two fuselage-mounted Vickers Mk V guns and a pair of either Lewis or Vickers guns which were carried in a streamlined blister fairing under the lower wing and fired clear of the propeller disc. But the definitive armament had not been established. It was still a suck-it-and-see operation. Therefore, the first thirty-seven aircraft of the second 180 production batch of Gladiator MkIs had Lewis under-wing guns, while the next ten aircraft carried Vickers K gas-operated guns in this position. The rest of the batch, when BSA production got underway, had four of the new Browning guns which became the standard armament. In order to fit these guns in the earlier production aircraft a special under-wing mounting to accept all the gun types was fitted. These were fired pneumatically, the 'safe-fire' twist button being located at the top of the control column's spade grip.

Gladiator MkII

Following increased demand by the RAF for Gladiators in the Middle East, a substantial number of modifications were embodied to create the Gladiator MkII to meet Specification F.36/37 given to Gloster in February 1938. The major changes were to the power unit and the cockpit instrumentation. The Bristol Mercury MkIX and its wooden propeller were replaced either by an 830hp Mercury MkVIIIA or MkVIIIAS supercharged engine, both turning a Fairey-Reed three-blade, fixed-pitch metal propeller. The VIIIA had a manual boost override, which allegedly provided an extra 10hp at altitude. The VIIIAS engine, which had Hobson mixture control boxes and semi-automatic boost-control carburettor to achieve maximum fuel economy, was among those built under the new 'shadow factory' scheme, hence the suffix 'S'. The Air Member for Research and Development, Air Marshal Sir Hugh Dowding – with a future war in mind – described the scheme as 'selecting an established manufacturer and then trying to create a replica of its production process somewhere away from the "parent" factory'. However, Gloster's shadow factory in Brockworth was only 300 yards from its Hucclecote parent.

Having been test-flown in a Gladiator MkI, the new cockpit display ran the gamut of instrument manufacturers by including a blind-flying panel carrying a Smiths airspeed indicator, Kollsman altimeter, Sperry artificial-horizon and directional gyro, Hughes rate-of-climb indicator and a Reid and Sigrist turn-and-slip indicator. An engine-driven vacuum pump served elements of this instrumentation and a cockpit electric engine-starting system was embodied. Other modifications for Middle East operations included a Vokes carburettor air-intake filter and desert equipment storage points. Despite an increase in loaded weight, the Gladiator MkII's airfield performance, climb, endurance, range and maximum speed were noticeably better than those of the MkI.

Sea Gladiator (Interim) and Sea Gladiator

Although single-seat fleet fighter aircraft such as the Nimrod equipped some Royal Navy carriers during the 1920s and 1930s, the Royal Navy's policy seemed to be aimed at acquiring multi-role types which could undertake a range of offensive operations. The Skua, described as a two-seat general-purpose reconnaissance fighter which operated in the dive-bombing role, was the flavour of the time. However, its handling characteristics needed some grooming and production was delayed; thus, in 1937, the Admiralty realised that its lack of a dedicated fleet fighter had opened up a nasty gap in fleet defences. The Fulmar was ordered to fill it, but by 1938 a more immediate solution suggested was to create a naval version of the Gladiator which was in full production for the RAF.

Such was the Royal Navy's haste to get its hands on these fighters, the first thirty-eight airframes of the initial batch of fifty of the latest Gladiator MkIIs to come off the Hucclecote production lines in mid-1938 were retained by Gloster for airframe naval modifications. These included the addition of a tubular member under the bottom longerons just aft of the cockpit, with pivot points for a V-arrester hook. A Royal Navy TR9 radio and an airspeed indicator reading in knots were also fitted. In this form, delivery of these aircraft – now designated Sea Gladiator (Interim) – was completed during December 1938.

The main Sea Gladiator order of June 1938 was met by the first sixty aircraft out of a production batch of 300 Gladiator MkIIs. All the Sea Gladiators were delivered by mid-February 1939. By then the need for further modifications had been identified. These included external stowage of the pilot's emergency dinghy, which was located under the front-fuselage section aft of the undercarriage. The dinghy, which had an 800lb buoyancy, was carried in a two-piece duralumin container, its joints being fabric-sealed against water and petrol. Its side ropes had three sea markers and distress signals. The bottom of the container was connected to the cockpit by a cable and the dinghy could be deployed by pulling a handle located at the base of the control column. In addition, catapult strong-points were built into the airframe structure and the internal spent-ammunition cases and links-collector boxes were removed. They were replaced by long chutes to eject cases and links overboard clear of the dinghy pack. Mercury VIIIA and VIIIAS engines with three-blade metal propellers were standard fit on both Sea Gladiator variants. During January and February 1939 the first production Gladiator MkI, K6129, was flown at Naval Air Station (NAS) Worthy Down and the A&AEE on development trials. Provision also was made for the mounting of two additional Browning guns under the upper-wing root just outboard of the wing/centre-section joint. Although this installation was cleared for six gun firing in April, it was not embodied before Sea Gladiators were withdrawn from front-line service.

Gladiator Squadrons in Peacetime

The Air Ministry's principal reason for ordering the Gladiator was to provide RAF squadrons with an aeroplane which could 'hold the fort' until the new eight-gun monoplane fighters became operational. It was anticipated that Hurricanes would be well established in squadron service by early 1937; however, delivery dates began to slide down the calendar and it was not until January 1938 that 111 Squadron began to receive Hurricanes in substantial numbers.

Clearly, there was great concern in the minds of the Ministry's top brass that Gloster should deliver on time. As an insurance policy a batch of Hawker Fury MkIIs was also ordered at the same time as the Gladiator, even though the two-gun Fury's performance was generally inferior.

Meanwhile, during the autumn of 1936 production of the first batch of twenty-three Gladiator MkIs was under way at Hucclecote – the manufacture of all major components being completed before final assembly began. Initial check flights on the first three production aircraft, K6129–6131, were undertaken in January 1937; then, on 22 February five pilots from 72 Squadron, led by Flight Lieutenant E.M. 'Teddy' Donaldson, arrived at Hucclecote to collect K6130-6134 and ferry them to RAF Church Fenton in Yorkshire. The rest of the squadron's Gladiators were delivered during the following two weeks. During its conversion to Spitfires at Acklington in March–April 1939, it converted back to Gladiators for several weeks because the airfield surface didn't suit the Spitfires. Many of the other aircraft in this first production batch replaced Bulldogs in 3 Squadron during March. The Gladiator's service with this squadron almost began with the bang of an accident. As the first one took off from Hucclecote for Kenley, its engine stopped; however, the RAF pilot quickly switched fuel tanks and was able to make a successful landing back at Hucclecote. This squadron later converted to Hurricanes but after a fatal crash with one of them it also converted back to Gladiators because RAF Kenley was now reckoned to be a bit too small for the 'Hurris'. It got its Hurricanes back again in May 1939 at Biggin Hill. A small number of this first production batch of Gladiator MkIs was retained for trials at the A&AEE and, later, for Sea Gladiator development.

On 27 April 1937 54 Squadron at Hornchurch became the first to re-equip with Gladiators having the universal under-wing gun mounting able to accept Vickers, Lewis and the new Browning guns, these aircraft coming from the second production batch of 180 Gladiator MkIs. Among other squadrons equipping in 1937 were 65 Squadron which, from 1 June, was equipped with second-batch Gladiator MkIs while at Hornchurch, flying them principally in the night fighter role; a week later the first Browning-armed Gladiators joined 73 and 87 Squadrons at Debden with 56 Squadron at North Weald equipping in July with new and 'second-hand' aircraft from other squadrons. All were Essex-based airfields.

During the rest of the year these squadrons took part in various air exercises. On 26 June their Gladiators appeared in the RAF Pageant at Hendon attacking a 1924-vintage Virginia bomber; then, three days later, Gloster test pilot Michael Daunt flew a factory-new aircraft at the SBAC show at Hatfield. By early autumn 1937, all eight Gladiator squadrons were operational. Then, on 17 October, the *Luftwaffe* came to Croydon. On foot. This was a reciprocal visit by the Germans, a group of very top brass RAF officers – including Air Vice Marshal Courtney, Deputy Chief of the Air Staff – having visited Germany the previous January. Now Major-General Ernst Udet, Lieutenant-General Stumpf and General E. Milch led a party of senior *Luftwaffe* officers who visited several key aircraft and engine factories and five RAF stations. At Hornchurch, an important airfield in the London defences, they inspected 54 and 65 Squadron's Gladiators and saw

Following engine trials at the A&AEE this Gladiator I, seen at Hucclecote, was shipped to 4 Aircraft Delivery Unit in the Middle East in July 1937.

Before being flown by three RAF squadrons Gloster used this Gladiator I, K7968, for trials with Vickers gas-operated under-wing guns.

Four 72 Squadron Gladiator MkIs and pilots rest from practicing their routine on 25 June, rehearsal day for the 1937 RAF Display at Hendon. Note the parachute packs on the tailplanes.

them in the air. Less than two years later the *Luftwaffe* came again, this time at altitude and being met by Hurricanes and Spitfires. Head on.

During the winter months of 1937–38 a number of Gladiators were lost in crashes, several after the aircraft could not recover from flat spins. Some ex-Gauntlet pilots bemoaned the loss of its sensitive control characteristics and having to come to terms with the use of flaps. In addition the aircraft was being criticised as a gun platform. Over-speeding of the Watts two-blade propeller in a dive created airframe vibration and pilots were unable to hold their gun-sights firmly on a target. Bristol Aeroplane's Roy Fedden solved the problem by suggesting a different reduction gear ratio for the Mercury engines. The results were approved in the squadrons. Gradually these and other snags were overcome and Gloster then claimed: 'The aeroplane provides a very steady gun platform and adjustment of the guns is simple and easy. Particular attention has been given to ease of maintenance on the ground. The guns, ammunition boxes and cartridge chutes are readily accessible and removable.' Clearly, the company was aiming to please both the pilots and the armourers!

By March 1938 a number of Gladiator squadrons were beginning to receive Hurricanes. The first was 3 Squadron, its Gladiators being shipped to storage in Egypt, while 56 Squadron's aircraft replaced Demons in 25 Squadron at Hawkinge. However, on 10 July, there was a final piece of 'skylarking' by three Gladiators of 87 Squadron at a great French Fête de l'Air at Villacoublay. The pilots, Sergeant Dewdney, Pilot Officer Lorimer and Flying Officer Feeney, in spite of low cloud and drizzle, demonstrated their own outstanding skill and the Gladiator's handling qualities by flying a tied-together aerobatic display with the cords linking them attached to their aircraft's interplane struts.

The first squadron to move to Ismailia, Egypt was 80 Squadron arriving in May 1938, joining 33 Squadron to form a Gladiator Wing for the defence of the Suez Canal region. Formed at Khormaksar, Aden, with some Sea Gladiators (Interim) taken over from the Navy, 94 Squadron provided air cover for the port while 112 Squadron collaborated with a Blenheim squadron and other local defence forces.

But already the rattling of sabres in Germany could be heard in Whitehall with Adolf Hitler threatening to annexe Czechoslovakia in pursuit of his demands of 'greater living space' for Germans. On 30 September 1938 Prime Minister Neville Chamberlain returned from the last of three meetings with Hitler in Munich seeking a peaceful answer to this situation in Europe. As he stepped from a British Airways Lockheed 14 at Heston Airport he waved a small piece of paper, later stating his belief that it was 'peace in our time'. He was wrong; however, his appeasement policy was to buy an invaluable extra year of peace during which the RAF prepared for war.

Within a week or so the 'Munich Crisis' was over; nevertheless, Fighter Command was strengthened by an intake of Auxiliary Air Force (AuxAF) squadrons equipped with Gladiators given up by RAF units. In March 1939, 607 Squadron at Usworth was the first, making its air gunners redundant by swapping its Demon two-seat fighters for 25 Squadron's Gladiators; 54 Squadron passed its Gladiators to 603 Squadron AuxAF, some ex-56 Squadron's aircraft wound up with 604 Squadron AuxAF and numbers of 605 Squadron's Gladiators had previously been flown by three other squadrons. Throughout the rest of 1938 and into 1939 all Fighter Command squadrons concentrated on air-combat exercises as the AuxAF units were integrated with the Regular squadrons. Meanwhile, from about the middle of 1938, Gladiators of 33 and 80 Squadrons had been 'operational' in the Suez Canal region with detachments in at least five other Middle East locations.

Thirty-eight Sea Gladiator (Interim) aircraft were taken on Admiralty charge, thirteen being delivered to NAS Worthy Down and the remainder to Donibristle, Fife, Hatston on Orkney and Eastleigh, with some being crated for delivery to stores in Malta. Four Sea Gladiators began sea trials in the carrier HMS *Courageous* in March 1939 with the first squadron, 801 with six aircraft, embarking in May and 802 finally having six Sea Gladiators aboard HMS *Glorious* a few months later. In the Mediterranean by September 1939 a crated batch of eighteen Sea Gladiators had arrived in Malta.

Gladiator Squadrons at War

France 1939–1940

For Great Britain the Second World War began on Sunday, 3 September 1939, with Neville Chamberlain announcing on the radio at 11 a.m. that '…this country is at war with Germany'. Ten minutes later the air-raid sirens wailed, but it was a false alarm. On that day RAF Fighter Command's Order of Battle listed thirty-nine home-based squadrons of which eighteen had replaced their ageing biplanes with Hurricanes and Spitfires, but still included four first line AuxAF Gladiator squadrons; they were 603 605, 607 and 615 Squadrons stationed at Turnhouse, Tangmere, Usworth, and Kenley. Within a few weeks 152 Squadron formed at Acklington and 263 Squadron at Filton, both were equipped with Gladiators.

During early September squadrons patrolled the north-east and south coasts. It was 8 October when three 607 Squadron's Gladiator MkIs, up from Acklington, spotted a Dornier 18 twin-engined flying boat. They attacked and forced it down; later its crew were taken prisoner. Then, on 15 November, 607 and 615 Squadrons, with a mixed bag of a dozen transport aircraft, flew from Croydon to Merville in France, about twenty-five miles south of Dunkirk. From there, as part of the Air Component of the British Expeditionary Force (BEF) they patrolled the area until Merville's grass airfield became unserviceable and they moved to Vitry-en-Artois. During the early months of 1940 both squadrons scored victories in the intermittent air battles. Then in May, as they gave support to the BEF, which was withdrawing to the coast ports for evacuation, the Gladiators were overwhelmed by almost continuous bombing attacks. Finally, around 21 May, all surviving personnel were evacuated back to England where 615 Squadron received replacement Gladiators. They flew patrols from Manston, covering the fleets of small craft helping to bring back some 300,000 men of the BEF off the Dunkirk beaches. 607 Squadron then converted to Hurricanes.

Norway 1940

Meanwhile, 263 Squadron – having been scrambled on earlier occasions from Filton in defence of Bristol – sailed from Scapa Flow for Norway aboard the carrier HMS *Glorious*, arriving on 24 April 1940. Sea Gladiators of 802 and 804 Squadrons Fleet Air

Sea Gladiator N2276 of 803 Squadron gets airborne from HMS *Furious* without its dinghy in 1940.

One of fifty Gladiators converted to Sea Gladiators during production, N5517 demonstrates its arrester hook. It joined 801 Squadron in HMS *Courageous* for trials in 1939.

Arm provided fighter cover for *Glorious* en route to Norway. Meanwhile 263 Squadron's task was to support British and Norwegian ground forces battling against the invading German army and the *Luftwaffe*. The following day the frozen Lake Lesjaskog was initially used as a base but, by evening, it had been heavily bombed and the ice shattered with aircraft sinking through it and others damaged. Despite many courageous sorties that day by 263 Squadron's pilots, who shot down six enemy aircraft, relentless bombing attacks by Heinkel 111s virtually destroyed all the Gladiators on the ground. On 28 April the RAF contingent returned to Scotland in a cargo ship.

During the first three weeks of May 1940 a second contingent arrived in Norway with 263 Squadron's Gladiator MkIIs, which arrived aboard HMS *Glorious*, and were based at Bardufoss. Already, German forces were proving too strong for the Allied armies in Norway and on 2 June an evacuation was ordered. Again, heavy attacks by *Luftwaffe* bombers could not be totally beaten off although numbers of them were downed by Gladiators. During one afternoon sortie Pilot Officer Jacobsen destroyed three Heinkel 111s and damaged a Junkers 88. While the ground crews returned home by a cargo ship, 263 Squadron's pilots, and some from 46 Squadron with Hurricanes, flew their surviving aircraft onto *Glorious* again, though none had arrester hooks. Tragically, on 8 June, the aircraft carrier and two attendant destroyers were sunk by the German battle-cruisers *Gneisenau* and *Scharnhorst* with the loss of all but two of the RAF pilots. During these two gallant expeditions Gladiator pilots destroyed fifty enemy aircraft for the loss, in air combat, of only two pilots and their aircraft.

The Mediterranean 1940–1941

By early 1940, Malta, a small but vital Mediterranean base, had become the holder of Sea Gladiators for passing aircraft carriers which re-equipped with them for shipping protection duties and for delivery to other bases. In addition, carrier-borne Sea Gladiators

N5628, a Gladiator MkII, was flown by 263 Squadron in Norway. It was lost when the frozen Lake Lesjaskog was bombed. Recovered from the lake in 1968, its remains are in the RAF Museum. Note the Gloster-built Hawker Henley behind it.

Gladiator MkII, N5628, seen with 263 Squadron in Norway in April 1940. The three-bladed metal propeller and the nearby 'trolley-acc' engine starter are noteworthy.

gave air support to convoys and to Swordfish torpedo-bombers in actions against Italian warships including the renowned strike at their base at Taranto on 11 November 1940. In April 1940 four stored Sea Gladiators were assembled on Malta to form a Fighter Flight to defend Hal Far Airfield; two more were later put together and stationed at Luqa.

On 10 June, Italy declared war on the Allies, and the Sea Gladiators had difficulty in intercepting the fast *Regia Aeronautica* bombers with their fighter escort, which immediately attacked Valetta's dock area. The RAF pilots' tactics were then directed at disrupting the bombers' aim. It proved effective. One of the Sea Gladiators was fitted with two more Browning guns under the top wings, the only known six-gunned Gladiator. However, it never flew, being destroyed on the ground. The few Gladiators attacked large enemy formations daily and gradually their numbers were diminished until only three were airworthy. During the first five weeks of the war against Italy these three aircraft, plus a few Hurricanes, had intercepted seventy-two enemy formations and destroyed thirty-seven of their aircraft. When more Hurricanes arrived to strengthen the Island's defences just two Sea Gladiators remained serviceable.

Reference must be made to the alleged naming of three Sea Gladiators *Faith*, *Hope* and *Charity*. Most reliable sources report that these names were first used by a journalist some time after Sea Gladiators were operational in Malta.

Western Desert June–October 1940

Three days after Italy entered the war, 33 Squadron was out strafing enemy aircraft at Sidi Aziz and scoring victories in air combat with *Regia Aeronautica* aircraft. Offensive

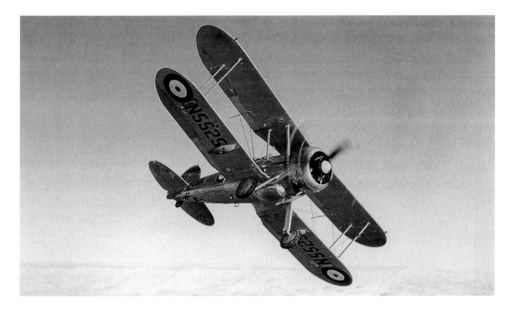

This Sea Gladiator, N5525, was among eight shipped to Malta in crates to provide spares. Here it shows off its ventral dinghy pack between its landing gear legs.

In April 1940 Sea Gladiator N5519 was among the first batch to be taken on charge by RAF Malta. It has a three-blade metal propeller and retains the arrester hook cradle.

Radio Mechanic Charles Bell checks the equipment in Sea Gladiator N5528 in Malta.

A Gladiator MkII of 112 Squadron and its ground crew seen, in the Western Desert region, possibly at Sidi Haneish, during the late summer of 1940.

operations continued in conjunction with 80 Squadron until 33 Squadron returned to Egypt to fly patrols over Alexandria then gave up its Gladiators to a RAAF squadron having destroyed fifty-eight enemy aircraft in the air and on the ground. At one time 80 Squadron was somewhat divided having one flight with the Army and another re-equipping with Hurricanes; however, one of its Gladiator pilots brought down an Italian bomber. In July 1940, 112 Squadron had moved to the Western Desert in support of Allied ground forces before going to Greece in January 1941 to join 80 Squadron.

Eastern Mediterranean

Following Italy's unprovoked attack on Greece during 1940, in November 80 Squadron moved to a base in north-west Greece near to the border with Albania and found that the *Regia Aeronautica* aircraft were easy targets, destroying eleven bombers and fighters on their first patrol without loss. One flight, led by Flight Lieutenant Edward Gordon Jones, operated from Trikkala in central Greece. Gordon Jones scored three victories before being shot down, but destroyed two more after recovering from bullet wounds. Total victories numbered around forty by the end of the year. In January 1941, 112 Squadron arrived in Greece and almost immediately knocked down eleven Italian aircraft. But a few weeks later the *Luftwaffe* began to join the Greek campaign and its end loomed ominously. In March 80 Squadron converted to Hurricanes and withdrew to Crete with 112 Squadron which gave its Gladiators to a Greek Air Force squadron

L8025, one of the RAF's Gladiator MkIs which were transferred to the Royal Egyptian Air Force in the spring of 1939.

in June when it withdrew to Egypt. The number of Gladiators and Sea Gladiators still airworthy in Crete could be counted on the fingers of one hand. Three eventually returned to Egypt.

A notable Gladiator pilot was South African Flight Lieutenant M.T.St.J. Pattle DFC. He was credited with more than thirty enemy aircraft destroyed, a substantial number of them while flying Gladiators.

Aden 1940–June 1941

Operating in defence of Aden against the threat of attack by *Regia Aeronautica* aircraft in Somaliland – which included flying boats – 94 Squadron's Gladiators, plus some Sea Gladiators, were flown on a variety of missions with great success. They included an attack on a surfaced Italian submarine which was then captured by a tug; the destruction of an Italian fuel dump and aircraft in Ethiopia as well as several bombers. A South African Air Force unit took over this squadron's Gladiators in April 1941.

By this time there were no operational Gladiator squadrons in the Middle East Air Forces. However, when RAF Habbaniyah in Iraq was besieged by rebel Iraqi forces, a small group of Gladiators was collected and flown to the scene where it flew standing patrols to ward off further air attacks. On one of these patrols a Heinkel 111 was shot down, as was a Fiat CR.42 biplane fighter during another patrol.

During the Second World War a total of twenty-eight RAF squadrons and fifteen Meteorological (Met) flights plus nine First Line and twelve Second Line Fleet Air Arm squadrons flew Gladiators and Sea Gladiators.

Gladiators in other Colours

In March 1937 a Latvian Air Mission was in Britain seeking to buy military aircraft for its air force. At Hucclecote a Gladiator MkI was displayed for them and on 27 May an order for twenty-six aircraft with Vickers MkVM 7.7mm guns was received. The cost of £120,000 nicely covered the Gladiators plus three Hawker Hind light bombers. The money was raised through a State lottery.

Only a few days after Gloster received the Latvian order, Lithuania ordered fourteen Gladiator MkIs. After being test flown they were dismantled, crated and shipped during October and November 1937 and assembled at air bases at Vilna and Kaunas. Following the occupation of Latvia and Lithuania by Russia and Germany, their Gladiators are known to have been flown in the markings of these two occupying powers during the Second World War.

Norway became attracted to the Gladiator I in April 1937 when initial discussions with Gloster centred round an order for six Gladiator MkIs followed by licensed production of the type in Norway. The initial order was for twelve aircraft, but when six had been delivered to Fornebu, near Oslo, the contract was revised in July 1938 and six Gladiator MkIIs were taken from an Air Ministry contract and delivered to Norway. During July

Gloster and Hawker pilots, and one dog, with a group of Belgian Air Force pilots at Hucclecote in October 1938 before the delivery flight of a squadron of Gladiators to Belgium.

A ski-equipped Gladiator of the Swedish Volunteer Unit seen with Finnish markings in early 1940.

1940, armed with four Colt .300in guns, the remaining nine serviceable Gladiators took part in defending Oslo against heavy *Luftwaffe* air attacks. By the end of the month all were destroyed – either in combat or on the ground – where several were abandoned after breaking through the ice of frozen lakes being used as air strips. Before this they had destroyed at least four enemy aircraft.

In 1937 plans for expanding the Royal Swedish Air Force (RSAF) included buying fifty-five Gladiators, the first thirty-seven being Gladiator MkIs. These aircraft were designated J8s in RSAF service. Deliveries began in June and about nine months later eighteen Gladiator MkIIs, designated J8As, were ordered. These were powered by 740hp Mercury VIIs – licence built by *Nohab Flygmotorfabriken* at Trollhatten – driving three-blade metal propellers. Of these, forty-five aircraft were allocated to the three squadrons which formed 8 Fighter Wing and ten aircraft were held in reserve. This fighter wing was formed in July 1938 at Barkarby near Stockholm. As part of a Swedish volunteer force, which gave aid to Finland in the war with Soviet Russia, the fighter wing went into action in January 1940. Large numbers of their Gladiators had Swedish-made ski undercarriages and could carry four lightweight bombs under each wing. Over a two-month period, three Gladiators were lost but the fighter wing operated successfully against Russian bombers, destroying twelve of them while loosing two Gladiators. Gladiators remained in frontline service with the RSAF until spring 1941.

Following Russia's attacks on Finland in November 1939, thirty ex-RAF Gladiator MkIIs were taken from stocks in the UK and, during the next three months, were shipped in small batches to Finland. These aircraft formed part of the fighter defences of the southern region of that country. When that campaign ended in March 1940 half the Gladiator force had been lost.

An order for twenty-two Gladiator MkIs from Belgium was met with deliveries starting on 12 September 1937 and continuing until May 1938, but plans for licensed production by Avions Fairey in Belgium never materialised. Gladiators were operated by the Belgian Air Force until the middle of 1940, by which time it is believed that most of them had been destroyed in combat with enemy aircraft.

In October 1937, when China and Japan were at war, thirty-six Gladiator MkIs were ordered by the Chinese Government. The crated aircraft went by rail and then by junk up the Pearl River and thence to Tien Ho – 'River in the Sky' – airfield. Once there a Gloster working party of engineers assembled at least four of them in the open, despite attacks by Japanese aircraft. The rest of the first twenty Gladiators were assembled during December 1937 and January 1938 at Bai Yuen – 'White Cloud' – Airfield and on open sites, including a roadway and a graveyard. They were then flown some 300 miles away where training could begin without interference from Japanese air attacks.

As part of a re-equipment programme involving British aircraft, in 1938 the Irish Air Corps acquired four new Gladiators MkIs. These were flown from Hucclecote to Baldonnel where they served until 1941.

In January 1938 a wealthy Greek business man, Zarparkis Homogenos, bought two Gladiator MkIs from Gloster and presented them to the Royal Hellenic Air Force (RHAF). His £9,400 bill included a quantity of ground equipment and spares. During the latter end of 1940 at least thirteen RAF Gladiator MkIIs were transferred to the RHAF by 33 and 80 Squadrons when they re-equipped with Hurricanes, plus four more from stocks held by RAF Middle East.

A Portuguese Government order received in February 1939 with a request for quick delivery of fifteen Gladiator MkIIs was met by switching aircraft from an Air Ministry contract. A proposed order for thirty additional Gladiator MkIIs never arrived at Gloster.

Eighteen Gladiator MkIs converted to MkII standard were handed over by the RAF to the Royal Egyptian Air Force (REAF) during March/April 1939. Some were returned to the RAF and modified for use by Met Flights. This pattern of transfer and recovery of RAF Gladiators was repeated in 1941 when twenty-seven Gladiator MkIIs were handed over to the REAF.

Drawing on RAF Middle East stocks, between 1940 and 1942 nine Gladiator MkIs were transferred to the Royal Iraqi Air Force. Five Gladiator MkIIs followed them in 1944, two remaining airworthy until 1949.

After a solitary Gladiator MkI from 72 Squadron was transferred to the South African Air Force in January 1939, eleven Gladiator MkIIs followed them in April 1941. These were flown operationally and for training by 1, 2 and 3 Squadrons SAAF in the Middle East and East Africa.

Soviet and Luftwaffe Gladiators

Following the declaration of Latvia as a Soviet Socialist Republic in 1940 and its later occupation by German forces during the Second World War, a number of Latvian Air Force Gladiators were seized and taken to Russia and Germany where they were flown in Soviet and German markings. The similar sequence of events occurred in neighbouring Lithuania at about the same time. Little information has emerged about the subsequent history of those flown in Soviet markings although at least two, in fairly good condition, are recorded as having been flight-tested before ending up in a wreckage-strewn aircraft dump.

The *Luftwaffe* put their Gladiators to good use, at least nine appearing on the strength of *Erganzungsgruppe* (S)1 during 1942–43. Stationed at Langendiebach near Frankfurt this 'Supplementary Group' was a training unit for glider pilots destined to fly the DFS 230 troop-carrying glider. This role was indicated by the letter 'S' for '*Segelflugzeug*' [glider] in this group's designation. It was here that the Gladiators earned their corn as glider tugs, having been modified with a towing bridle under the rear-fuselage aft of the tailwheel. No doubt a cable-release system was also installed in these aircraft. Records show that the Gladiators listed on the group's register were designated and numbered Gloster G1, G2 and so on, and carried *Luftwaffe* markings, for example NJ+BO. Also recorded was a list of Gladiator glider tugs which crashed or were involved in accidents, including four having sustained major damage or had been written off between March 1942 and March 1943.

Gladiator Production Data

A total of 747 Gladiators was produced by Gloster Aircraft Company Ltd at Hucclecote, Glos:

Gloster SS.37	One prototype	K5200
Gladiator MkI	378 aircraft	K6129–6151, K7892–8055, L7608–7623, L8005–8032
plus 147 exports to Latvia, Lithuania, Norway, Sweden, Belgium. China, Eire and Greece.		
Sea Gladiator (Interim)	38 aircraft	N2265–2302
Gladiator MkII	12 aircraft	N2303–2314
Sea Gladiator	60 aircraft	N5500–5549, N5565–5574
Gladiator MkII	258 aircraft	N5575–5594, N5620–5649, N5680–5729,
		N5750–5789, N5810–5859, N5875–5924

Total includes 18 built for Sweden and 21 aircraft switched from Air Ministry contracts to Norway (N5919–5924) and Portugal   N5835–5849

MkIs transferred	44 aircraft to Greek, Egyptian & Iraqi Air Forces
MkIIs transferred	49 aircraft to Greek, Egyptian, South African & Iraqi Air Forces

Gloster Gladiator MkI data

Powerplant: One 830hp Bristol Mercury MkIX nine-cylinder, supercharged, air-cooled radial engine turning a 10ft-diameter Watts wooden two-blade propeller.

DIMENSIONS:

Length	27ft 5in
Wingspan	32ft 3in
Tail-down height over vertical propeller	10ft 9in
Wing area top	169.2sq.ft
Wing area bottom	153.75sq.ft
Aerofoil section	RAF 28
Chord	5ft 9in
Dihedral	3 degrees
Aspect ratio	6.44
Stagger	2ft 3in
Aileron movement – Total	6.75in
Maximum flap angle	90 degrees
Tailplane area	19.3sq.ft
Tailplane incidence movement	3.3 degrees up – 4 degrees down
Elevator area	18.25sq.ft
Elevator movement	10.25in up – 9.0in down
Fin area	5.9sq.ft
Rudder area	14.5sq.ft
Rudder movement	19 degrees each way

WEIGHTS:

Structure, control surfaces, undercarriage	1,723lb
Powerplant and associated system components	1,494lb
Armament and synchronising system:	
Radio	350lb
Electrical equipment	135lb
Oxygen and cockpit heating systems	49lb
Instrumentation	39lb
Miscellaneous equipment	11lb
Total Equipment	584lb
Pilot and parachute	200lb
Fuel (70 gallons)	539lb
Oil (5 gallons)	45lb

Normal all-up weight   4,585lb

Normal all-up weight with Fairey metal propeller   4,640lb

WING LOADING

Normal all-up weight Watts/Fairey propeller   14.2/14.4lb/sq.ft

PERFORMANCE:

LEVEL SPEED:

Altitude	TAS/mph
Sea Level	210
5,000ft	226
10,000ft	245
14,500ft	253
17,500ft	250
20,000ft	235

CLIMB:

To altitude	Time
10,000ft	4.66min
20,000ft	9.05min

SERVICE CEILING:

(Rate of climb 1,000ft/min)	32,800ft

TAKE-OFF AND LANDING:

Take-off run	375ft
Take-off run to clear 50ft	600ft
Landing distance from 50ft	510ft
Stalling speed, flaps up/down	56/53mph

ENDURANCE:

With full load and 70 gallons of fuel	96 minutes

RANGE:

As above condition	352 miles

Gloster Gladiator MkII data

As for Gladiator MkI except following data:

POWERPLANT:

One 830hp Bristol Mercury VIIIA or VIIIAS nine-cylinder, supercharged, air-cooled radial engine turning a 10ft 6in-diameter Fairey Reed three-blade fixed-pitch metal propeller.

DIMENSIONS:

Tail-down height over vertical propeller	10ft 7in

WEIGHTS:

Structure, control surfaces, undercarriage	1,810.6lb
Powerplant and associated system components	1,633.6lb
Other equipment fit similar to Gladiator MkI	1,420lb
Normal all-up weight	4,864.2lb
Wing loading	15.1lb/sq.ft

PERFORMANCE

LEVEL SPEED

Altitude	TAS/mph
Sea level	215
5,000ft	224
10,000ft	249
14,600ft	257
17,500ft	253
20,000ft	239

CLIMB

To altitude	Time
10,000ft	4.5min
20,000ft	8.75min

SERVICE CEILING:

(Rate of climb 1,000ft/min)	33,500ft

TAKE-OFF AND LANDING:

Take-off run to clear 50ft	540ft
Landing distance from 50ft	750ft
Stalling speed flaps up/down	57.5/54.5mph

ENDURANCE

With full load and 70gallons of fuel	90min

RANGE:

As above condition	340 miles

GLOSTER SEA GLADIATOR DATA

As for Gladiator MkII except following data:

WEIGHTS:

Structure, control surfaces, undercarriage	1,880.1lb
Powerplant and associated system components	1,673.2lb

OTHER EQUIPMENT FIT SIMILAR TO GLADIATOR MKI

and MkII includes dinghy pack and arrester hook	1,466.2lb
Normal all-up weight	5,019.5lb

PERFORMANCE:

LEVEL SPEED:

Altitude	TAS/mph
Sea level	210
5,000ft	220
10,000ft	245
14,600ft	253
17,500ft	248
20,000ft	230

CLIMB:

To altitude	Time
10,000ft	4.66min
20,000ft	9.0min

SERVICE CEILING

(Rate of climb 1,000ft/min)	32,200ft

TAKE-OFF AND LANDING:

Take-off to clear 50ft	320ft
Landing distance from 50ft	780ft
Take-off deck (30kt wind)	195ft
Stalling speed flaps up/down	58/55mph

ENDURANCE:

With full load and 70 gallons of fuel	80mins

RANGE:

As above condition	320 miles

RAF Gladiator Squadrons

3 Squadron
Received Gladiator MkIs in March 1937 at Kenley. In March 1938 converted to Hurricanes but reverted to Gladiators in July. Moved to Biggin Hill in May 1939, reverting to Hurricanes in July

6 Squadron
An Army co-operation squadron with a 'backing group' of fighters, in August 1941 at Wadi Halfa, Sudan, it supplemented Hurricanes with Gladiator MkIIs until January 1942 when Blenheims had arrived.

14 Squadron
While converting from Wellesleys to Blenheims at Port Sudan, in September 1940, a flight of Gladiator MkIs was taken on strength for an unidentifiable but short time.

25 Squadron
Forsook its two-seat Demons while at Hawkinge in June 1938 and took over
56 Squadron's Gladiator MkIs. It exchanged them for Blenheims in February 1939.

33 Squadron
Reformed on 1 March 1938 at Ismailia, Egypt with Gladiator MkIs which it took to Palestine. Moved to Western Desert in September 1939 re-equipping with Gladiator MkIIs

at Mersa Matruh, Egypt, in March 1940. Converted to Hurricanes in September at Helwan, Egypt.

54 Squadron
Reformed at Hornchurch on 15 January 1930. It converted from Gauntlet MkIIs to Gladiator MkIs in April 1937, exchanging them for Spitfires in March 1939.

56 Squadron
Disbanded a few weeks earlier at Aboukir, Egypt but reformed at Hawkinge on 1 November 1922. Exchanged Gauntlet MkIIs for Gladiator MkIs during July 1937 at North Weald, converting to Hurricanes in April 1938.

65 Squadron
Reformed at Hornchurch on 1 August 1934 it exchanged Gauntlet MkIIs for Gladiator MkIs in May 1937 converting to Spitfires in March 1939.

72 Squadron
Reformed at Tangmere with Gladiator MkIs on 22 March 1937. Converted to Spitfires in April 1939, temporarily flew Gladiators throughout March 1940, then returned to Spitfires.

73 Squadron
Reformed at Mildenhall on 15 March 1937 flying Furies until Gladiator MkIs arrived in June at Debden. A year later it re-equipped with Hurricanes.

80 Squadron
Reformed at Kenley on 8 March 1937 with Gladiator MkIs. Moved to Ismailia, Egypt in May 1938 and, with 33 Squadron, formed Gladiator Wing for defence of Suez Canal region. Operated in Western Desert and Greece until March 1941 until evacuated to Crete and then Palestine. Re-quipped with Hurricanes three months later.

85 Squadron
Reformed from 'A' Flight 87 Squadron at Debden on 1 June 1938 with Gladiator MkIs and converted to Spitfires in September.

87 Squadron
Converted from Fury MkIIs to Gladiator MkIs in June 1937 at Debden and began to receive Hurricanes in July 1938.

94 Squadron
Reformed at Khormaksar on 26 March, 1939, as Aden's aerial defence force maintaining a 24-hour battle flight with Sea Gladiators. In 1940 it was equipped with Gladiator MkIs and MkIIs, flying them until June 1941 when Hurricanes arrived.

112 Squadron

Formed in HMS *Argus* leaving Portsmouth for the Middle East on 16 May 1939. At Helwan, Egypt received Gladiator MkIs and MkIIs before seeing action in the Sudan, Western Desert, Greece and Crete from where it was evacuated to Egypt in June 1941. Converted to Tomahawks in July.

123 Squadron

In April 1942 it parted company with its Spitfire Vbs at Castletown and flew Gladiator MkIIs in October/November in Egypt until Hurricanes arrived.

127 Squadron

Reformed at Habbaniya, Iraq, from 'F' Flight of 4 Service Flying Training School on 29 June 1941 with Gladiator MkIs and MkIIs and some Hurricanes. It relinquished its Gladiators in July.

141 Squadron

At Turnhouse, on 4 October 1939, 141 Squadron reformed with Gladiator MkIs and the squadron worked up at Grangemouth until succeeded by Defiants in April 1940.

152 Squadron

Reformed at Acklington on 1 October 1939 and for three months flew fighter-training sorties in Gladiator MkIs and MkIIs until getting Spitfires in December.

247 Squadron

On 1 August 1940 reformed at Roborough from the Sumburgh Fighter Flight which had flown Gladiator MkIIs in defence of the Shetlands. Became operational as 247 Squadron two weeks later for the defence of Plymouth. This was the only Gladiator unit in Front Line Service on 8 August 1940, the start of the Battle of Britain. It converted to Hurricanes in December.

261 Squadron

Reformed on 1 August 1940 from the Malta Fighter Flight with four Sea Gladiators. In July 1941 Gladiator MkIs joined the squadron which received Hurricanes by September.

263 Squadron

Reformed at Filton on 20 October 1939 with Gladiator MkIs and MkIIs for defence of Bristol and the South West. Went to Norway in HMS *Furious* during April 1940, operating from frozen Lake Lesjaskog. Evacuated on April 26 but returned to Norway in May. On 8 June re-joined HMS *Glorious*, which was sunk that day.

274 Squadron

On 19 August 1940 the 274 Squadron reformed at Amriya, Egypt, with Gladiator MkIIs but exchanged them for Hurricanes almost immediately.

603 Squadron
Changed from light bombers to a fighter squadron at Turnhouse on 24 October 1938 being wholly equipped with Gladiator MkIs by March 1939. In August it began receiving Spitfires.

604 Squadron
During May 1940, while operating Blenheims in the night-fighter role at Manston, it began flying Gladiator MkIs. In the same month its Gladiators were replaced by Beaufighters.

605 Squadron
A light bomber squadron, converted to fighters on New Year's Day 1939, equipping with Gladiator MkIs and MkIIs. From September it maintained readiness at Tangmere with Gladiators until completely equipped with Hurricanes in November.

607 Squadron
Flew Gladiator MkIs from March 1939 at Usworth. In November moved to France as part of the air component of the BEF. Operated from Merville, Vitry-en-Tardenoise, Abbeville and Bethune until May 1940 before converting to Hurricanes in June.

615 Squadron
An Army co-operation squadron, it converted to fighters on 7 November 1938, exchanging its Gauntlets for Gladiator MkIs at Kenley in May 1939 and Gladiator MkIIs in October. In November to France with the BEF operating from Merville, Vitry-en-Tardenoise, Poix and Abbeville with detachments until May 1940, converting to Hurricanes in April 1940.

FLEET AIR ARM GLADIATOR SQUADRONS

759 Squadron
Formed at Eastleigh on 1 November 1939 as a Fighter School and Pool Squadron. Aircraft included four Sea Gladiators and became a Fleet Fighter School. Moved to Yeovilton in September 1940 and had relinquished its Gladiators by April 1943.

760 Squadron
Having formed at Eastleigh on 1 April 1940 as Fleet Fighter Pool No.1, it had one Sea Gladiator on strength which remained with the squadron for only five months.

767 Squadron
Formed at Donibristle on 24 May 1939 as Deck Landing Training Squadron. Sea Gladiators taken on strength in April 1940.

769 Squadron
Formed at Donibristle on 24 May 1939 with training in HMS *Furious*. Four Sea Gladiators detached to form 804 Squadron on 30 November. This squadron disbanded on 1 December 1939.

770 Squadron

Two Sea Gladiators were among initial equipment when formed at Lee-on-Solent as a Deck-Landing Training Squadron on 7 November 1939. Embarked in HMS *Argus* it moved to the Mediterranean and was based at Polyvestre, France. Disbanded on 1 May 1940.

771 Squadron

A Fleet Requirements Unit which formed at Portland on 24 May 1939, it received Sea Gladiators in December and retained at least one until June 1944.

775 Squadron

Formed at Dekheila, Egypt, in November 1940 as a Fleet Requirements Unit, during 1941 it had two Sea Gladiators in its fleet, retaining them until 1944.

776 Squadron

A Fleet Requirements Unit formed at Lee-on-Solent on New Year's Day 1941, it got Sea Gladiators twelve months later and flew them until June 1942.

778 Squadron

Following its formation at Lee-on-Solent as a Service Trials Unit Squadron, it flew Sea Gladiators from December 1941 to March 1943.

787 Squadron

Formed at Yeovilton as a Fleet Fighter Development Unit on 5 March 1941; equipped with some Sea Gladiators which it relinquished in November 1942.

791 Squadron

An Air Target Towing Unit, Sea Gladiators joined it in March 1942. The squadron disbanded in December 1944.

797 Squadron

Formed as a Fleet Requirement Unit at Katukurunda, Ceylon, in July 1942, a few Sea Gladiators were flown, then it was relinquished during 1943.

800 Squadron

In October 1938 Gladiator MkI, K8039, joined this squadron aboard HMS *Courageous* during A&AEE Sea Gladiator development trials, remaining with it until February 1939.

801 Squadron

Embarked in HMS *Courageous* from February to May 1939 Sea Gladiators served in this Deck Landing Training Squadron while equipping with Skuas.

802 Squadron

This Fleet fighter squadron re-equipped with Sea Gladiators in May 1939 and embarked in HMS *Glorious* for Mediterranean service. In April 1940 they participated in two expeditions by Allied forces in Norway. Ceased to exist from 8 June when HMS *Glorious* was sunk by two German battle cruisers.

804 Squadron

With four Sea Gladiators from 769 Squadron this shore-based fighter squadron was formed at Hatston on 30 November 1939. Embarked in HMS *Glorious* for the first expedition to Norway, providing continuous patrols over the Royal Navy fleet. The Sea Gladiators were phased out in January 1941.

805 Squadron

Reformed at Akrotiri on New Year's Day 1941, some Sea Gladiators joined Fulmars for the defence of Crete in March but were withdrawn in June.

806 Squadron

Formed as a fighter squadron on 1 February 1940 at Worthy Down, in August it embarked for the Mediterranean in HMS *Illustrious* with a small number of Sea Gladiators which, with Fulmars, provided cover for Allied forces in Crete but were exchanged for Hurricanes in May 1941.

813 Squadron

Sea Gladiators joined the squadron in June 1940 aboard HMS *Eagle* operating in the Mediterranean. They were withdrawn in March 1941.

880 Squadron

A Fleet fighter squadron which formed at Arbroath on 15 January 1941, it flew three Sea Gladiators until June when they were succeeded by Sea Hurricanes.

885 Squadron

Formed at Dekheila, Egypt, on 1 March 1941 with six Sea Gladiators, it embarked in HMS *Eagle* and was disbanded on 1 May.

Other Fleet Air Arm Sea Gladiator-equipped Units

Station Flights: RNAS Crail 1943; RNAS Inskip 1943; RNAS Henstridge 1943.
For several years after being withdrawn from front-line service Gladiators were still being flown on communication duties, as station 'hacks' and on 'Met' flights in the UK and overseas until 1944.

RAF Gladiator Meteorological Flights

401/1401 Flight
Formed as 401 Meteorological Flight from the RAF Meteorological Flight on 2 February 1941 at Mildenhall with two Gladiators. From 1 March 1941 all 400 Squadron series flights became 1400 Squadron series. Re-formed as 1401 at Manston and then converted to Spitfires.

402/1402 Flight
Originally part of the Air Ministry Met Flight, which received Gladiators in May 1939, this flight was formed on 15 January 1941 at Aldergrove, Ulster. Converted to Hurricanes from July 1944. The last Gladiator served until January 1945.

403/1403 Flight
Formed at Bircham Newton as 403 Met Flight in November 1940. Reformed at North Front, Gibraltar, in May 1943 with Gladiator MkIIs for Temperature and Humidity (THUM) recording flights. Re-designated 520 Squadron in September 1943.

1411 Flight
Formed as a Met Flight at Heliopolis, Egypt, with Gladiator MkI and MkIIs for data recording for Palestine and Egypt. On 1 January 1942 re-designated 1411 Flight operating over Western Desert region. Re-equipped with Hurricanes in July 1943.

1412 Flight
Formed on 14 April 1941 as Met Flight 1412 at Khartoum, Sudan, on 21 September 1941 with four Gladiator MkIs and MkIIs. Re-designated 1412 Flight on 1 January 1942.

1413 Flight
Formed as Met Flight at Ramleh, Palestine, with Gladiator MkIs on 21 September 1941. Became 1413 Flight on 1 January 1942 and began flying Hurricanes in July 1943.

1414 Flight
In December 1941 formed at Eastleigh, Nairobi, with four Gladiator MkIs and MkIIs before converting to Hurricanes.

1415 Flight
Formed at Habbaniya, Iraq, on 18 July 1942 with six Gladiator MkIs and received Hurricanes in November 1943.

1560 Flight
Formed as a Ground Met Observation Flight on 6 December 1942 at Maiduguri, Nigeria, with three Gladiator MkIIs. Re-equipped with Hurricanes in April 1944.

1561 Flight

This Met Flight was formed on 1 May 1943 at Ikeja, West Africa. It flew Gladiator MkIIs until re-equipped with Hurricanes in April 1944.

1562 Flight

Formed at Waterloo, Sierra Leone, with three Gladiator MkIIs on 3 February 1943. In June 1944 converted to Hurricanes.

1563 Flight

Formed as a Met Flight with three Gladiator MkIs at 23 Parachute Training Centre, Helwan, Egypt, on 22 December 1942. In September 1943 it was re-equipped with Hurricanes.

1565 Flight

Formed with two Gladiator MkIs at Nicosia, Cyprus, on 1 February 1943, before-equipping with Hurricanes in May 1944.

1566 Flight

Formed on 1 February 1943 at Khormaksar, Aden, flying Gladiators. In May 1944 re-equipped with Hurricanes.

1567 Flight

Formed with Gladiator MkIs and MkIIs and Hurricanes at Khartoum, Sudan, in June 1943. Re-equipped with Spitfires in July 1945.

520 Flight

Formed from 1402 Met Flight at Gibraltar on 20 September 1943 and equipped with Gladiator MkIIs and Hudsons in the same role. Converted to Spitfires and Halifaxes in June 1944.

521 Flight

Formed on 1 August 1942 at Bircham Newton from 1401 and 1403 Flights as a Met Calibration Squadron flying several different aircraft types. Gladiator MkIIs remained in service until March 1945.

Other Gladiator Squadrons

Fighter Flight, Shetlands, formed on 18 December 1939 with three Gladiator MkIIs plus two reserve aircraft from 152 Squadron at Turnhouse. Re-named Fighter Flight, RAF Sumburgh on 5 January 1940. Moved to Roborough to form 247 Squadron on 1 August 1940 with Gladiator MkIIs.

16 Flight

An Army Co-operation squadron it flew Gladiator MkIIs and Lysanders from May to September 1940 with the BEF from Bertangles, France.

18 Flight

In May 1940 this light-bomber squadron, which withdrew from France to West Raynham with Blenheims, had Gladiators for airfield defence duties.

237 Flight

Originally 1 Squadron Southern Rhodesian Air Force, it was re-numbered in April 1940. It flew Gladiator MkIIs on tactical reconnaissance duties from March to August 1941 in the Sudan and Egypt.

267 Flight

Re-forming on 19 August 1940 at Heliopolis, Egypt, as a communications and transport unit, in March 1941 it acquired a Met Flight with four Gladiators, retaining them for most of that year.

Among other RAF Gladiator-equipped units were: No.1 Air Armament School, Manby 1940; RAF School of Army Co-operation, Old Sarum, 1943; Nos 2 and 26 Anti-Aircraft Co-operation Units, Middle East, 1938; Nos 1622, 1623 and 1624 (Anti-Aircraft Co-operation) Flights 1943; Air Defence Co-operation Unit, Ismailia 1942; No.3 Air Observers School, Bobbington 1941; Communications Flight, Iraq 1944; Communications Unit, Western Desert, 1942; Reserve Echelon Fighter Flight, Prestwick, 1940; K', 'Q'and 'X' Flights Special Defence Duties, Sudan, India, Palestine, Iraq 1940, 1941, 1942; Nos 13, 29 and 201 Group Communications Flights, Ouston, Dumfries, Mariut 1940, 1942, 1943; Nos 4 and 9 Flying Training Schools, Habbaniya, Hullavington, 1939, 1940; No.10 (Observers) Advanced Flying Unit, Dumfries, 1942; No.1 Practice Flying Unit 1940 and Telecommunications Flying Unit, Hurn, 1941.

NINE

REPAIR AND RESTORATION

Marshall of Cambridge Ltd at Teversham, one of the forty-four companies in the wartime Civil Repair Organisation, had its own private air defence force. Responsible for repairing and overhauling Gladiators, its test pilot, Peter May, acquired some ammunition during the Battle of Britain and kept two armed Gladiators available for 'flight-testing' during air-raid warnings. This was to encourage the workforce to continue on their jobs during these warnings. On three occasions during 1940 the Gladiators took off but no enemy aircraft appeared. As the Gladiators lacked radio the pilots watched the local buses, which stopped during the warning periods. When the buses moved again they knew the 'all-clear' had sounded and the aircraft could land.

The Shuttleworth Collection's Gladiator, L8032/G-AMRK, holds the record for airworthiness. Delivered by road to No.27 Maintenance Unit at Shawbury on 4 October 1938 where its Mercury engine was installed, it was then taken on charge by numerous units.

In the autumn 1943 a batch of Gladiators returned to Hucclecote to be overhauled before going on to Met Flights. Don Underwood, a Bristol Aeroplane engine-service engineer told the author:

> I remember going to Gloster's factory to do some work on those Gladiators. We exchanged a few cylinders and other components on the Mercury engines without taking them off the aircraft. There were about a dozen but we didn't work on all of them. Some were test flown by a Gloster pilot but a few were stored.

Was L8032 among them? It was finally struck off Air Ministry charge and acquired by Gloster Aircraft on 23 February 1948. By then it had logged only eighty flying hours during its nine years in RAF service.

For a long period L8032, and another Gladiator, N5903, had been parked in Gloster's flight shed and erecting shop, allegedly still waiting for their overhaul and new meteorological equipment to be fitted. Then, in November 1950, this author arranged their transfer by road transport to two Air Service Training Ltd establishments; L8032 went to Hamble and N5903 to Ansty for use as ground-trade instructional airframes. When Ansty closed the following year, N5903 was moved to Hamble where in 1951, Vivian Bellamy, an ex-Fleet Air Arm Gladiator pilot, bought them for £5 each.

At Eastleigh, where Bellamy's company 'Flightways' was based, he created an airworthy Gladiator by swapping engines and other equipment during a major restoration of L8032. He first flew it in the spring of 1952 with the civil registration G-AMRK and attended a number of air displays. However, he discovered that maintaining and flying an elderly military aeroplane was extremely costly and he offered to sell it back to Gloster Aircraft; thus, this author negotiated G-AMRK's purchase by the company for £200 and welcomed it back to Hucclecote on 20 August 1953. A lack of components affected its serviceability; only careful welding and patching enabled the exhaust collector ring, for example, to survive. A letter to *The Aeroplane* and *Flight* magazines from Gloster's ex-chief test pilot, Eric Greenwood, (then the company's Technical Sales Manager and the author's boss) had appealed for information on 'the whereabouts of one of these Mercury 8 collector rings'. Several months later Air Traffic Control at RAF Lyneham telephoned the author and reported that an Iraqi Air Force transport aircraft had off-loaded a large packing case addressed to Gloster Aircraft. It contained an unused collector ring in perfect condition.

In 1957, Dickie Martin, then Gloster's chief test pilot, inspired a group of apprentices and some ex-employees to undertake another restoration programme on G-AMRK. With Air Ministry approval, it was given RAF markings and those of 72 Squadron plus the serial number K8032. It was flown by Martin and Geoff Worrall – later chief test pilot. With the impending closure of the company, K8032's future was uncertain. Then, on 7 November 1960, it was handed over to the Shuttleworth Collection, along with a handsome dowry, by Hugh Burroughes, a founding director of Gloster Aircraft Co. Then Dickie Martin made the last take-off of a Gloster aeroplane from Hucclecote that day. Since then it has appeared in countless air displays where the sight and sound of this veteran aeroplane and its engine and propeller have stirred memories for thousands upon thousands of spectators.

In 1974, K8032 got some new fabric which, with the help of ex-Gloster employees, was applied by Flight One, aircraft-maintenance engineers, at Staverton, now Gloucestershire Airport. When the wings were removed it was found that the port upper wing differed from the other three. It had Sea Gladiator camouflage and part numbers were completely different. Furthermore, it had a mouse's nest in the leading edge. Probably built when the wing was in store, its inhabitant's urine had done a good job corroding the nose ribs, which had to be replaced. As no tiny skeletons were found it was presumed that they had quit the nest before the wing was airborne and anoxia had ended their days.

And what happened to the original and genuine RAF Gladiator MkI, K8032, whose identity was usurped by L8032? Built in 1937 it flew with 73 Squadron at Debden, with 3 and 615 Squadrons at Kenley, moved on to 605 Squadron at Castle Bromwich and Tangmere, and to 263 Squadron at Filton. It was then shipped to storage on RAF Middle East charge.

In August 1968 members of the RAF College's sub-aqua club began diving operations in Lake Lesjaskog in Norway. Their aim was to recover the remains of some of 263 Squadron's Gladiators which had sunk through the lake's bomb-shattered ice some twenty-eight years earlier. Their initial dives, using only snorkel equipment, were disappointing but later attempts discovered two airframes. Choosing the more complete one, even though its longerons were fire-damaged and corroded, they attached three inflatable dinghies to it which, it was hoped, would lift the airframe when they were

Left: L8032/G-AMRK comes back to Hucclecote in August 1953. Vivian Bellamy steps out of the Gladiator for the last time with the author (right) and J. Scoble, Flight Department chief inspector, to receive them.

Below: Gloster Aircraft apprentices and their instructors who carried out a lot of the refurbishing and engineering work on G-AMRK.

With the engine roaring two apprentices, ropes in hand, wait ready for Dickie Martin's signal to pull away the Gladiator's wheel chocks seconds before its last flight from Hucclecote.

On 7 November 1960 Hugh Burroughes, Gloster Aircraft's chairman, formally presented the Gladiator, K8032, to Air Commodore Alan Wheeler, a Trustee of the Shuttleworth Collection, standing behind him. Ted Shambrook, financial director and Dickie Martin, chief test pilot (holding the scroll) also took part.

Ted Currier's splendid photograph of K8032 taken on 13 May 1962 at RAF Upavon's Open Day marking the fiftieth anniversary of the founding of the Royal Flying Corps.

inflated. Sadly, one dinghy blew out of its securing ropes and one became inverted, then the fuselage broke where the longerons were damaged. However, the remainder was lifted by a dinghy attached to the engine's lifting-eye and it was dragged into shallow water with ropes around the landing gear, with the tail being raised soon afterwards. With time running out, they stripped off the port upper wing and other equipment, one piece of which carried the serial N5628, which was crated with the airframe and flown to the UK. The front fuselage of Gladiator MkII, N5628, is now in the RAF Museum at Henlow. A complete Gladiator MkI, K8042, is also in the Battle of Britain Hall at the Museum.

It is difficult to allocate serial numbers to all the Gladiators and components recovered from Lake Lesjaskog and other Norwegian sites but, as this book is being written, at least twelve Gladiators and Sea Gladiators or their major airframe elements are either on display or being restored in the UK, Norway, Sweden and Malta, with two in an airworthy condition. Among them are: K8042, at Battle of Britain Hall, RAF Museum, Hendon; Sea Gladiator National War Museum, Fort St Elmo, Valetta, Malta, carries serial N5520 and name *Faith*; N5628, ex-263 Squadron is at the RAF Museum, Hendon; N5641, ex-263 Squadron is at the Norwegian Air Force Museum, (RNAFM) Bodo Air Base, Norway; N5643 is in Norway, a restoration for Armed Forces Museum, Oslo; N5719, ex-263 Squadron is situated at Retro Track & Air, Cam, Gloucestershire; it was recovered from mountains in Narvik, Norway, and has been restored to flying condition; N5903 is at Fighter Collection, Duxford, and restored to flying condition; Fv278 MkII Flygvapenmuseum, Malmslatt, Sweden, exhibits the ex-Royal Swedish Air

RAF College Sub-Aqua members, Flt Cadets Rees and Proctor, with the tail section of N5628 being raised to Lake Lesjaskog's surface.

Flg Off P. Gates, SAC A. Gray and Flt Cadet Proctor, with 'look what we've found' expressions, hold Gladiator MkII N5628's tail section at the lake's edge.

Despite twenty-eight years under water in Lake Lesjaskog these Gladiator components were found only 6ft down. A wing-mounted gun fairing with the serial number N5632 and part of the rudder are among them.

Force Gladiator, J8A. There are other Gladiator restoration programmes in the UK and Norway. In addition, quantities of Gladiator airframe components and equipment have been recovered from Norway including N5628, N5632, N5638, N5647, N5693, N5704, N5705, N5905 and N5907.

Gladiator Colour Schemes

During its operational life RAF Gladiators and FAA Sea Gladiators carried several different paint schemes and markings. These are the principal ones: Prototype and production Gladiators had an overall aluminium/silver finish and black serial numbers. In peace-time service they generally carried individual multi-coloured squadron insignia. Wheels, fins and spinners were sometimes coloured to identify different flights or squadron and flight leader's aircraft. In 1938 the upper surfaces were dark green and dark earth camouflage, the port lower-wing under surface was night black and starboard lower-wing under surface was white; under surface of tailplane and fuselage aft of wings was aluminium/silver; squadron code letters were sea grey with black serial numbers. It is said that the night black/white scheme was to aid recognition by the Observer Corps (later Royal Observer Corps) during pre-war exercises.

Gladiator G-AMRK seen in flight over the Severn Valley in 1954 having been bought by Gloster and displayed in these markings for some two years.

K8032, with 72 Squadron RAF markings, climbs away from Hucclecote on its history-making last flight of a Gloster aeroplane from that airfield on 7 November 1960.

The 1940 models' upper surfaces – except lower wing and areas in shadow – were dark green and light green, dark earth and light earth; upper surfaces of lower-wing fuselage sides, under upper-wing and lower-fuselage sides were light green and light earth; under surfaces were aluminium/silver; sea grey medium-squadron code letters and black serials. The design and size of RAF roundels on wings and fuselage constantly changed with at least five different ones being applied.

Sea Gladiator

In 1938, early production Sea Gladiators had an overall aluminium/silver finish with Air Ministry-type roundels and black serials. Between 1938 and 1940 later Sea Gladiators carried similar camouflage schemes employing dark slate grey, which had a green tint, and extra-dark sea grey on upper surfaces and dark sea grey and light-slate grey for those in shadow. The RAF night/white scheme for lower-wing under surfaces was used but later changed to sky grey and then to sky. Roundel size and design also changed. Different schemes were applied to suit other Air Forces' requirements

During the 1960s the fuselage of Malta's Sea Gladiator, which has been given the serial N5520, was craned out of The Armoury in one of Valetta's narrow streets for storage elsewhere.

The basic structure of Malta's Sea Gladiator can be seen through the multiplicity of ropes used during its exit from the Armoury.

RAF Luqa's volunteer team who carried out the first refurbishment of the Sea Gladiator in 1974. From the left are Cpl Rajah, Sgt Feeney and Chief Technician Alcock.

This close-up photograph shows the rather harsh paint scheme and the given name *Faith*, one of the three mythical Malta Sea Gladiators, under the windscreen.

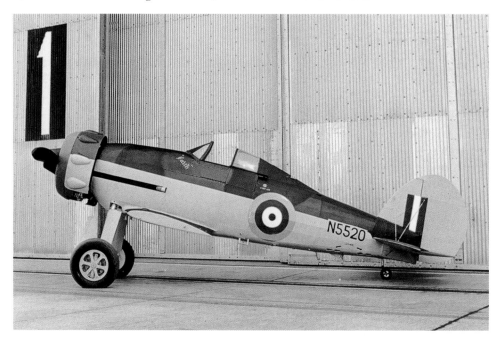

The result of RAF Luqa's refurbishment programme outside one of the station's hangars.

The Sea Gladiator in use as a 'chariot' at RAF Luqa for Group Captain M.J. Armitage, Station Commander, as he leaves that station to return to the UK. The 'horses' are Officers Mess members.

Flying the Gladiator

New Zealander Wing Commander Al Deere, renowned Battle of Britain fighter pilot, was very forthright in his comments about flying the Gladiator. Having served for a year with 54 Squadron when equipped with Gladiators at RAF Hornchurch in 1938, it is recorded that he said: 'Thank God we didn't have to fight in Gladiators. It was a lovely aircraft but it was so outdated'. He went on to say that, fortunately, when war came he was flying Spitfires.

A Gloster chief test pilot who, in addition to flying Meteors and Javelins, also flew the Shuttleworth Trust's Gladiator, Geoff Worrall, has more than forty single-, twin- and four-engined types in his log book. Almost all tail-draggers, they include the P-47 Thunderbolt, Spitfire, Mustang, Auster, Dakota, Rapide, Anson and Heron.

Geoff recalled that:

It was on 19 May 1954 that our new chief test pilot, Dickie Martin, asked me to fly the Gladiator at a display. My first flight at Hucclecote, with other pilots, my wife Barbara and various Flight Shed staff in attendance, was not an unqualified success. Trouble with the fuel feed and carburettor shortly after take-off, followed by some expensive noises from the engine, led to a swift circuit and landing. But things got better after that.

As for the handling, Geoff says that:

It is a nice little aeroplane. When I flew it, it was a bit nose-heavy at lower speeds and I had difficulty landing trying to make a good three-pointer, I generally just trundled it in. The controls were generally well harmonised, manoeuvrability was very good and the visibility was good for a biplane. We flew her carefully, she's an old aeroplane. The Mercury started easily and ran well and was very economical. I logged about forty hours in the Gladiator. It is not as pleasant to fly as a Spitfire – what could be – but I suppose you can't compare a biplane with a monoplane.

A big thrill was joining with a Meteor NF.14 and Javelin F(AW)4 from 72 Squadron for a photographic sortie with Gloster's photographer Russell Adams on 11 June, 1959. This was to celebrate the re-equipment of the squadron with its third Gloster fighter, the Javelin. I flew the Gladiator, with its 72 Squadron markings, up from Gloster's Moreton Valence airfield to RAF Church Fenton. We took off from there and Russell got his pictures off Flamborough Head in East Yorkshire, not on the South Coast as some 'experts' have claimed.

Wing Commander Vivian Owen-Jones, O.C. of 72 Squadron flying the Javelin, set course from Church Fenton for Flamborough Head at about 180 knots, Squadron Leader Ian Hawkins in the Meteor joined up with him and I slotted in from a gentle dive. Russell in a Meteor T7 came alongside to get the photographs. The Javelin pilot wasn't too keen to be flying so slowly at low level and we flew in formation for only a short time before returning to Church Fenton. It was dusk when I landed and the ground crew, with the chocks, backed away when they saw blue flames, which were invisible in daylight, coming out of the old Mercury's exhaust pipes.

Three generations of Gloster fighters. The Javelin and Meteor are finding it difficult to fly at dangerously low speed to formate with the Gladiator.

Geoff Worral positions the Gladiator for Russell Adams in the two-seat Meteor T7 to get a photograph of K8032's top surfaces.

Air Commodore Alan Wheeler who flew Gladiators at the A&AEE and RAE once commented: 'If the Gladiator could be criticised at all, I might say that, flying it, one was perhaps conscious of beginning to lose that sense of being actually part of the machine. Fighters had, by then, started to get big.'

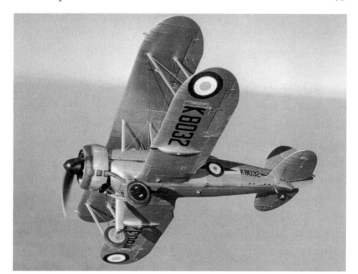

The Gladiator peels away
to show its underwing
armament.

Geoff Worrall, with a traditional leather flying helmet and sleeves rolled up, in Gladiator K8032. The windscreen, sliding canopy and hinged door are interesting features of this veteran fighter.

TEN

FOLLAND'S MONOPLANE FIGHTER

In 1935 while Folland's design team were still busy with modification work on the Gladiator MkIIs and Sea Gladiators, he and Howard Preston turned their attention to Specification F.5/34. This was another ambitious advance in fighter requirements which would lead to the Hawker Hurricane and Supermarine Spitfire. It called for a single-seat aeroplane with no less than eight guns, a 275mph maximum speed at 15,000ft, a service ceiling of 33,000ft and ninety-minutes' endurance. Designers were free to choose the engine. Vickers (Aviation) and Martin Baker Aircraft submitted monoplanes, as did Gloster.

For what would be the last time, a new Gloster aeroplane bore a striking resemblance to its predecessor. Some years earlier Harald Penrose, Westland Aircraft's chief test pilot, had referred to Folland's creation of the Gladiator as 'typical of the archaic evolutionary mode of aircraft design' he had used. One wonders what Harald thought of Sydney Camm's mode of design when, between 1925 and 1936, fourteen different Hawker aeroplanes were created by the evolutionary mode. Even so, Folland stuck to this method when designing his F.5/34 aeroplane. Dubbed the 'Gloster Unnamed Fighter', it was virtually an all-metal monoplane Gladiator. He had jettisoned the upper wing, designed a thicker lower wing to house the Dowty retractable main landing gear and eight guns while the Bristol Mercury air-cooled radial engine, sliding-cockpit canopy and tail unit were almost Gladiator lookalikes.

The fuselage was a monocoque structure with oval-section formers and heavier rings with strong-points for engine, wing and tail-unit attachment, all clad with a duralumin skin. The one-piece wing had tip-to-tip light-alloy spars and ribs interspersed with steel ribs. Control surfaces were fabric-covered. The main and tail landing-gear units retracted backwards, leaving a part of the wheels exposed under the wing and tail unit to protect them in the event of a wheels-up landing. The 840hp Mercury MkIX in a long-chord cowling drove a de Havilland three-blade metal propeller.

Construction of the F.5/34 prototype, serialled K5604, was slow because of on-going work with Gladiator development. Then, in January 1937, when this prototype was far from complete, Henry Folland resigned from Gloster Aircraft. His successor was W. George Carter, later to design the little E.28/39, Britain and the Allies' first jet aeroplane, and the Meteor; thus construction of the F.5/34 was completed under his control. Gerry Sayer, Gloster's test pilot, made the first flight in late December 1937, only a few days before 111 Squadron received the first of its Hurricanes. It was not until March 1938 that the second prototype F.5/34, K8089, first got airborne. At the A&AEE, while K5604's top speed was 316mph at 16,000ft and it climbed to that height in eight and a half minutes, these two aircraft failed to improve on the Hurricane's performance and, after being flown by the RAE as well, both became ground instructional airframes. A sad end to Henry Folland's last fighter.

Clearly, the design of Folland's F.5/34 'Unnamed Fighter' was based on the Gladiator but it produced a very clean and compact aeroplane. The landing gear looks too frail to support its two-and-a-half-ton all-up weight.

This photograph shows the unusual design of the deep main spar web which enabled the guns to be mounted inside the wing. Four blast tubes protrude through it, the guns firing through the leading edge of the tip-to-tip one-piece wing.

When retracted into the F.5/34's thick wing the big panels closed over the landing gear leaving part of the wheel protruding below it.

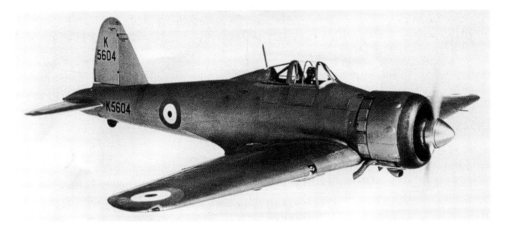

The first of the two F.5/34 prototypes has a pugnacious appearance in the air, even though there are no gun apertures in the wing. Part of the tailwheel remained unretracted in flight.

With K5604's engine running, Gerry Sayer talks to a mechanic, who is leaning into the cockpit, before a test flight at Hucclecote.

ELEVEN

FOLLAND AIRCRAFT CO. LTD

Why had Henry Folland resigned from Gloster Aircraft? Hugh Burroughes, who had been instrumental in attracting him to Gloucestershire Aircraft in 1921, told the author that, from late 1934, following the Hawker Aircraft take-over of the Hucclecote company, Folland did not relish the idea of working under the indirect control of the Hawker Board. He believed that it would favour the designs of Hawker's Sydney Camm, whose Furies had given him a leading position as a fighter designer. Folland gave Gloster outstanding service with two long, successful periods with the Grebe and Gamecock and then the Gauntlet and Gladiator. However, he had become worried and frustrated at his apparent inability to design a contract-winning aeroplane. Out of this mental turmoil came a great urge to have his own company where he could work unfettered by remote control from Kingston-on-Thames.

Soon after leaving Gloster, Folland, together with his talented assistant Howard Preston, moved to British Marine Aircraft at Hamble. Following that company's previous year's loss of £220,000, a complete new Board, which included him as technical director, had been appointed to reverse the company's fortunes. By December 1937 new contracts were in hand. Of major importance was the decision to change the company's name to Folland Aircraft. The Board believed that it would be advantageous as Folland was, by then, managing director. He was well known and trusted by the Air Ministry and foreign governments with a record of success as a designer during the previous twenty-five years.

The new name received Board of Trade Approval on 23 December 1937 and the company thrived on sub-contract work for many of the major aircraft manufacturers, particularly during the Second World War. Although some forty-five military and civil aircraft projects emanated from Hamble, only one was ordered. The Fo.108 was a flying-engine test bed of which twelve were built to Specification 43/37, the first one flying in late 1940. Although it had the Folland name, it bore no trace of that master designer's hand in its design. It was an ungainly aeroplane incorporating a metal fuselage, thick wooden wings and fixed-landing gear. Nevertheless it was 'fit for purpose' and could be fitted with a range of engines for test flying. Test observer Harold Parkin said: 'I recall the aircraft as being an ideal flying test bed from the ground engineer's and test observer's standpoint. There was always room to work and install our test equipment, whether it was in the area of the engine nacelle or the airframe.'

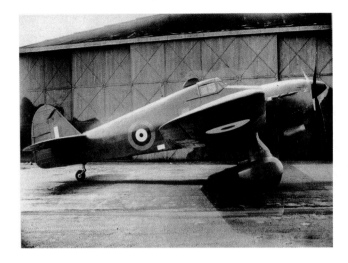

The first Folland Fo108 flying engine test bed, P1774, at Staverton in August 1941. It has a 2,000hp Napier Sabre liquid-cooled engine and three-bladed Rotol Airscrews propeller.

With its Sabre engine's cowling panels removed and wheels chocked the second Fo108, P1775, stands ready for ground engine running. Note the heavily enclosed fixed landing gear.

A long-chord cowling encloses a 1,700hp Bristol Hercules VIII air-cooled engine in P1775, minus its wheel spats, in March 1942.

Also seen in March 1942. P1775's lengthened cowling on the Bristol Centaurus engine seems cluttered with air intakes and an exhaust pipe.

'Now, that's low!' A Red Arrows pilot flew his Gnat down to head height for this dramatic photograph. The shadow on the ground indicates how low it was.

Folland Aircraft's Board of Directors in September 1950. From left to right: R.J. Norton, T. Gilbertson (general manager), W.E.W. Petter (deputy managing director), H.P. Folland (managing director), C.L. Hill (chairman), E.N. Egan (secretary), E.C. Lysaght.

Having launched the Company's Apprenticeship scheme, Henry Folland, OBE, took a great interest in his apprentices' training. He is seen here with Mrs Folland on 20 November 1951, when the apprentices made a presentation on 'the Boss's' retirement. From left, front row: Edward Petter, Henry P. Folland, Mrs Folland and T. Gilbertson.

Having had one break up in the air while he was flying it, Gloster test pilot Neil (always known as Michael) Daunt told the author: 'They were frightful aeroplanes with no stability. Bloody dangerous to fly'. It was he who dubbed the Fo108 the 'Folland Frightful'. Sadly, this name has stuck throughout the years.

Post-war sub-contract work kept the company busy, but in July 1951 severe ill health caused Henry Folland to resign as managing director, his successor being William Edward Willoughby Petter. Although unable to take a great part in the company's affairs, Folland remained on the Board until he died on 4 September 1954, just three weeks after the first flight of the Petter-inspired Folland Midge lightweight-jet-fighter prototype. One more aircraft bore Henry's name; this was the Folland Gnat.

Designed by Petter as a light, single-seat jet fighter, it was exported to India, where it was later built under license, and to Finland; however, it was developed and produced as a two-seat jet trainer for the RAF with whom it also became known worldwide as the aircraft flown by the Red Arrows formation-aerobatic team for some sixteen years.

Although the Hamble-based company which bore his name for several decades has had several owners and names, his was the hand which inspired and guided it throughout its early years, its vital wartime development and the complicated post-war period. The name Folland is written large in the history of Hamble-le-Rice. He is remembered, too, in Hucclecote, Gloucestershire, near to the site originally occupied by the Gloster Aircraft factories, where a side road 'Folland Avenue' leads, symbolically, to a small group of houses on roads named after Gloster's test pilots.